Contentious Identities

Daniel Chirot

It is often difficult to separate ethnic, religious, and nationalist identities as these frequently overlap. In today's world people's most important political identity and loyalty is to their nation, but that has only been true for at most a century or two. There continue to be serious conflicts in some states that are not nation-states between various ethnic, religious, and regionally based groups competing with each other for control of their states, or demanding independence as distinct nations. Even in most of what seem to be established nation-states there are ethnic, religious, or sometimes just regional minorities who are not fully assimilated into the national political culture. Intolerance or attempts to force minority communities into the nation is a prescription for conflict. There have been many cases of successful integration of culturally distinct communities into national wholes, and a majority of potential ethnic, religious, or nationalist conflicts actually get resolved or never even become contentious. Why some situations become conflictual, while others do not, and what can be done to mitigate conflicts where they occur are the main themes of this book.

Daniel Chirot is Job and Gertrud Tamaki Professor of International Studies at the University of Washington, Seattle. His books have been about genocide, ethnic conflicts, tyranny, social change, and Eastern Europe. He has consulted for NGOs, most recently for CARE in Africa. He has received a John Simon Guggenheim Fellowship and a Senior Fellowship at the United States Institute of Peace.

Framing 21st Century Social Issues

The goal of this new, unique Series is to offer readable, teachable "thinking frames" on today's social problems and social issues by leading scholars. These are available for view on http://routledge.custom gateway.com/routledge-social-issues.html.

For instructors teaching a wide range of courses in the social sciences, the Routledge *Social Issues Collection* now offers the best of both worlds: originally written short texts that provide "overviews" to important social issues *as well as* teachable excerpts from larger works previously published by Routledge and other presses.

As an instructor, click to the website to view the library and decide how to build your custom anthology and which thinking frames to assign. Students can choose to receive the assigned materials in print and/or electronic formats at an affordable price.

Body Problems
Running and Living Long in a Fast-Food Society
Ben Agger

Sex, Drugs, and Death
Addressing Youth Problems in American Society
Tammy Anderson

The Stupidity Epidemic
Worrying About Students, Schools, and America's Future
Joel Best

Empire Versus Democracy
The Triumph of Corporate and Military Power
Carl Boggs

Contentious Identities
Ethnic, Religious, and Nationalist Conflicts in Today's World
Daniel Chirot

The Future of Higher Education
Dan Clawson and Max Page

Waste and Consumption
Capitalism, the Environment, and the Life of Things
Simonetta Falasca-Zamponi

Rapid Climate Change
Causes, Consequences, and Solutions
Scott G. McNall

The Problem of Emotions in Societies
Jonathan H. Turner

Outsourcing the Womb
Race, Class, and Gestational Surrogacy in a Global Market
France Winddance Twine

Changing Times for Black Professionals
Adia Harvey Wingfield

Why Nations Go to War
A Sociology of Military Conflict
Mark Worrell

Contentious Identities

Ethnic, Religious, and Nationalist Conflicts in Today's World

Daniel Chirot

University of Washington, Seattle

NEW YORK AND LONDON

First published 2011
by Routledge
270 Madison Avenue, New York, NY 10016

Simultaneously published in the UK
by Routledge
2 Park Square, Milton Park, Abingdon, Oxon OX14 4RN

Routledge is an imprint of the Taylor & Francis Group, an informa business

Typeset in Adobe Garamond and Gill Sans by EvS Communication Networx, Inc.

Library of Congress Cataloging in Publication Data
Chirot, Daniel.
Contentious identities : ethnic, religious, and nationalist conflicts in today's world / Daniel Chirot. — 1st ed.
p. cm. — (Framing 21st century social issues)
1. Social conflict. 2. Ethnic conflict. 3. Culture conflict. 4. Group identity. I. Title.
HM1121.C48 2011
303.6—dc22
2010046663

ISBN13: 978-0-415-89200-1 (pbk)
ISBN13: 978-0-203-83419-0 (ebk)

Contents

Series Foreword

The world in the early 21st century is beset with problems—a troubled economy, global warming, oil spills, religious and national conflict, poverty, HIV, health problems associated with sedentary lifestyles. Virtually no nation is exempt, and everyone, even in affluent countries, feels the impact of these global issues.

Since its inception in the 19th century, sociology has been the academic discipline dedicated to analyzing social problems. It is still so today. Sociologists offer not only diagnoses; they glimpse solutions, which they then offer to policy makers and citizens who work for a better world. Sociology played a major role in the civil rights movement during the 1960s in helping us to understand racial inequalities and prejudice, and it can play a major role today as we grapple with old and new issues.

This series builds on the giants of sociology, such as Weber, Durkheim, Marx, Parsons, Mills. It uses their frames, and newer ones, to focus on particular issues of contemporary concern. These books are about the nuts and bolts of social problems, but they are equally about the frames through which we analyze these problems. It is clear by now that there is no single correct way to view the world, but only paradigms, models, which function as lenses through which we peer. For example, in analyzing oil spills and environmental pollution, we can use a frame that views such outcomes as unfortunate results of a reasonable effort to harvest fossil fuels. "Drill, baby, drill" sometimes involves certain costs as pipelines rupture and oil spews forth. Or we could analyze these environmental crises as inevitable outcomes of our effort to dominate nature in the interest of profit. The first frame would solve oil spills with better environmental protection measures and clean-ups, while the second frame would attempt to prevent them altogether, perhaps shifting away from the use of petroleum and natural gas and toward alternative energies that are "green."

These books introduce various frames such as these for viewing social problems. They also highlight debates between social scientists who frame problems differently. The books suggest solutions, both on the macro and micro levels. That is, they suggest what new policies might entail, and they also identify ways in which people, from the ground level, can work toward a better world, changing themselves and their lives and families and providing models of change for others.

Readers do not need an extensive background in academic sociology to benefit from these books. Each book is student-friendly in that we provide glossaries of terms for the uninitiated that are keyed to bolded terms in the text. Each chapter ends with questions for further thought and discussion. The level of each book is accessible to undergraduate students, even as these books offer sophisticated and innovative analyses.

In this contribution to the series, Daniel Chirot addresses the very timely issue of ethnic identity and ethnic conflict. His analysis ranges all over the globe, from the United States to Pakistan, Iraq, and Europe. He pays particular attention to the relatively recent concept of national identity, noticing that ethnic identity sometimes trumps national identity in salience especially where the national state may not have achieved full democratic maturity. This analysis is especially relevant as the United States plays an aggressive role in "nation building." Chirot's systematic analysis suggests that it is difficult to uproot people's ethnic identities, which have been sedimented over generations of struggle. Western social theory and social science need to address ethnic identity and conflict without sentiment or wishful thinking.

Preface

I began this small book intending to explain ethnic conflict. But in practice it is often difficult to separate ethnic, religious, and nationalist identities as these frequently overlap. In today's world most people's highest political identity and loyalty is to their nation, but that has only been true in a few European cases since the 1700s, and elsewhere more recently than that. Even today, it is not true everywhere. When we talk about ethnic conflict, we are really discussing disputes between different communities within a particular state. In the most severe cases, various ethnic groups question the legitimacy of the nation that claims to rule them, and either try to separate themselves or else to take over the state and establish a different kind of nation. To be sure, most ethnic conflicts are not nearly as severe as that, but that leads to one of the key question I wish to answer. Why do some potential ethnic conflicts never take place, while others are not very severe, and only a minority of them turn into violent encounters and sometimes outright war?

Many of the most prominent scholars of ethnic conflict say that the general public exaggerates its frequency precisely because in reality most potential ones never occur, but also because there are so many other sources of conflict that get confused with ethnic ones. This is true, but only up to a point. Competition over economic resources is a frequent source of internal conflict within states, but when the sides arrayed against each other identify themselves in ethnic terms, then a conflict is ethnic even if ethnicity as such is not the immediate cause of the dispute. Then there are regional conflicts, but again, if the contending sides identify themselves as distinct ethnicities, they become, in effect, ethnic conflicts. Ethnic groups that claim to have their own sovereign states become nations, or at least potential nations, so that ethnic and nationalist wars can amount to the same thing. This is equally true when the parties to the conflict identify themselves as different religious groups. Looking, for example, at the Catholic–Protestant conflict in Northern Ireland in the late 20th century, it is evident that it had almost nothing to do with theological disputes, but was really between two different ethnic groups that spoke the same language, lived in the same state, but rarely intermarried or socialized with each other, and were in many ways as segregated from each other as Blacks and Whites in the United States before the 1970s. In many cases, too, as between Israeli Jews and Palestinian Arabs, ethnic, national, and religious differences are so correlated with each other that it is impossible to say which are most important in fueling conflict. What counts is that two communities with very different identities are locked in a conflict over control of territory and resources, and they identify themselves differently on the basis of all three of these categories.

In other words, it is necessary to treat ethnic, religious, and national identities together, even though the differences between these categories are real enough, and can be analytically distinguished. Sometimes, only one or two of them are important, but in other cases all three exist together, and they are hard to separate in actual fact. What all have in common is that these identities can define particular communities that feel a sense of loyalty to each other and can be united for political objectives.

Though most of the world's population lives in fairly well established and solid nation-states, there continue to be serious conflicts in some states that are not nation-states at all, or only weakly so. In such places various ethnic, religious, and regionally based groups compete with each other for control of their state, or demand independence as distinct nations. Some of these cases are failed states, while others have simply been unable to convince all of the contending communities within their borders that they should owe allegiance to the state.

We cannot, however, overlook the fact that even in most of what seem to be solidly established nation-states there are ethnic, religious, or sometimes just regional minorities who are not fully assimilated into the national political culture, and this can lead to major political problems.

It is a major concern of this work to show that how minorities are treated, tolerantly or intolerantly, and what strategies are used to absorb or integrate them is a crucial determinant of whether or not conflicts actually break out, and when they do occur, how severe they become. This is a very important issue almost everywhere in today's world. We cannot hope to understand current political controversies ranging from race relations in the United States, to the treatment of Muslim immigrants in Europe, to religious violence in Iraq or Pakistan, to terrible civil wars in parts of Africa, and much else without better understanding the nature of identity-based conflicts. Intolerance or attempts to force minority communities into a nation is a prescription for conflict. There have been many cases of successful integration of culturally distinct communities into national wholes, and a large majority of potential ethnic, religious, or nationalist conflicts actually get resolved or never even become contentious. But when there is failure, the consequences are often dire. To understand our world we need to know why that sometimes happens.

1: From Family and Tribe to Modern Nation-State

Powerful group identities have always existed. Early humans' only group loyalties were to their families. Closely related groups of kin were crucial for survival, not only to deal with the physical environment, but also as protection against other groups of potentially competing kin-based groups. People identified with their group and it was within each one that critical decisions were made about resource allocation, how to provide for food, and what strategies to use to maintain security. Later, larger family groups, eventually **clans**, became the main focus of such **political** identities within which decisions were made that affected survival. At some point groups of clans formed **tribes**, which were larger groups that still considered themselves related in some ways. Today we might call these **ethnic groups** that shared a set of common values, a language, and a group identity that claimed a common set of ancestors, though in fact most such groups had ways of incorporating new arrivals who were not directly descended from those distant, often mythical ancestors. Part of the common set of beliefs or **culture** that these tribes or ethnic groups shared was religious—common gods, rules of behavior, and myths about creation and their place in their universe.

The Rise and Long Persistence of Agrarian States

It was only about 6,000 to 5,500 years ago, starting in and near what is today called Iraq, that the first **states** appeared. These were political groups governed by distinct classes of kings and priests protected by their own armies, able to tax their subjects in return for which they were supposed to insure their security from hostile tribes and neighboring states. The earliest states were small, typically based in fortified walled cities with a palace, a place to store grain that had been collected as taxes, and a temple complex designed to exalt the role of the rulers and reassure the population that they had divine protection. Temples and priests also served to make the ruling class legitimate by associating them with the gods.

In a sense these early states were like modern **nations**. Nations are groups of people who identify with and owe their primary allegiance to a particular state, or at least claim the right to have their own sovereign state. Whether they were formed by a single tribe, or an alliance of several previously self-governing clans or tribes who shared a common culture, the people in early states identified with their states.

Some states successfully created exceptionally effective armies that conquered other states and whole tribes or ethnic groups who did not share their own cultures. These were the early **empires**. By about 3100 B.C.E. Egypt had created a large, united kingdom. By about 2300 B.C.E. an equally large but much more multi-ethnic Sumerian Empire extended over what would later be called Mesopotamia (and is now Iraq). Later, large imperial states emerged in many other parts of the world, around the Mediterranean, in what is today northern India and Pakistan, in China, in Central America and Mexico, in the Andes mountains and valleys of South America, and in other places. These were no longer nations in any sense as they did not share entirely common cultures. They included people with different languages, religious ideas, and habits who were bound together by the force of the imperial state. In a few cases, notably in Egypt, these states held together long enough to create a more homogeneous culture and **religion**, so that they became something closer, again, to nations. China and some adjoining states that adopted much Chinese culture, namely Korea, Japan, and later Vietnam, also developed a common sense of loyalty and shared culture, but this was primarily among their **elites** who learned to read and write with Chinese characters, and this sense did not extend deeply into the body of commoners. Creating common cultures, even at the elite level, however, was a slow process that took many centuries, and many empires failed to do that.

During the more than 5,000 years from the creation of the earliest states and empires until roughly the 19th century a growing number of people lived in **agrarian states**. By about 2,000 years ago that already included the large majority of human beings. These states were agrarian because almost all of their people, in most cases 90 percent or more, were peasants who farmed the land and paid taxes to their lords, priests, princes, kings, and emperors. In almost all cases, difference between elites and common peasants created such a cultural gap that it was difficult for the majority of peasants to identify with the cultures of their rulers. Indeed it was common for agrarian states to be conquered by foreign states or tribes. This happened in the ancient world, where great empires such as Rome's ruled vast numbers of non-Latin speaking, non-Romans. At the top, elites might share the same language and set of values, but the overwhelming majority of rural commoners did not. Many of the great agrarian kingdoms and empires were repeatedly seized by nomadic tribes who then set up their own new states ruling over the previously settled peasant population.

This was not just ancient history. It happened often in China, whose empire was ruled as recently as 1911 by non-Chinese Manchurians who had conquered China in the 17th century. Until 1918 the Ottomans governed an empire whose majority was not Turkish. The Ottomans were descendants of a Turkish nomadic clan led by Osman (from which their name) that had established a state 600 years earlier and conquered a vast, non-Turkish population. For much of their empire's history,

amazon.co.uk

Thank you for shopping at Amazon.co.uk!

Billing Address
Department of Language & Linguistic
Science
University of York
Heslington
York, North Yorkshire YO10 5DD
United Kingdom

Shipping Address
Department of Language & Linguistic
Science
University of York
Heslington
York, North Yorkshire YO10 5DD
United Kingdom

Qty	Item		Our Price (excl. VAT)	VAT Rate	Total Price
1	**Contentious Identities: Ethnic, Religious and National Conflicts in Today's World (Framing 21st Century Social Issues)** Paperback. Chirot, Daniel. 0415892007 (** P-1-F104C160 **)		£7.99	0%	£7.99
	Shipping charges		£0.00		£0.00
	Subtotal (excl. VAT) 0%				£7.99
	Total VAT				£0.00
	Total				£7.99

Conversion rate - £1.00 : EUR 1,15

This shipment completes your order.

You can always check the status of your orders or change your account details from the 'Your Account' link at the top of each page on our site

Thinking of returning an item? PLEASE USE OUR ON-LINE RETURNS SUPPORT CENTRE.

Our Returns Support Centre (www.amazon.co.uk/returns-support) will guide you through our Returns Policy and provide you with a printable personalised return label. Please have your order number ready. (you can find it next to your order summary above). Our Returns Policy does not affect your statutory rights.

Amazon EU S.a.r.L, 5 Rue Plaetis, L-2338, Luxembourg
VAT number: GB727258821

Please note - this is not a returns address - for returns - please see above for details of our online returns centre

0/DKRyv8cVN/-1 of 1-//2ND_LETTER/econ-uk/6803353/0312 16:45/0311-16:57 Pack Type : A2

most Ottoman subjects were not even Muslims like the rulers, but various kinds of Christian ethnicities, including Greeks, Armenians, Serbs, and numerous others. The great central European Hapsburg Austro-Hungarian Empire that also lasted until 1918 included different ethnic groups, many of whom by the end were claiming their right to be independent, making the empire multi-national as well as multi-ethnic and multi-religious. The European colonial empires, and that of Japan that lasted into roughly the middle of the 20th century, were not nations. They were governed by modern nations but included vast numbers of people throughout the world who did not identify themselves as French, English, Japanese, Portuguese, or members of any other imperial state. The last great multi-national European empire was the Soviet Union, which ruled a large number of distinct groups that made up close to half of the state's population. Only in 1991 did this empire disintegrate, so that today, even though Russia remains multi-ethnic and multi-national, a large majority of those within its remaining borders do identify themselves as Russian, so that today Russia is finally more of a **nation-state** than an empire.

This story can be repeated for most of the world's states. At one time almost all agrarian states were ruled by elites who were either from culturally distinct backgrounds from most of their subjects, or who lived lives so different, richer, and more powerful than the majority of their subjects that there existed a huge gulf between the rulers and the ruled. England in 1066 was conquered by French-speaking Normans who were themselves descendants of Scandinavian Vikings who had conquered a piece of France a few centuries earlier, and the English aristocracy was more French than English speaking for a couple of centuries after that. The royal family of Thailand are partly descendants of Chinese who settled in Thailand, and both the royal families of Sweden and Spain were originally French. This happened long enough ago so that these royal families are now considered genuinely Thai, Swedish, and Spanish, but it was not always so. Even Japan's imperial family, long said by the Japanese to descend from the gods, are descendants of long-ago Korean invaders, something most Japanese nationalists fervently deny.

Religions as Exclusive Identities

All states strive for some sort of legitimacy, that is, they want their subjects to accept that it is right for those with power to possess it. Early states legitimized their rulers by associating them with the gods, and even deifying them by claiming that kings and emperors were either divine themselves, or at least graced by the gods and given mystical powers. But early religions tended to be very narrowly based. Each tribe had its own gods or favored god. Imperial states that incorporated many different tribes and ethnic groups devised different ways of combining these. The point was not to make all those different kinds of commoners part of the same nation, as that was not deemed possible in an age of mass illiteracy and poor communications, but to at least get them to recognize the sacredness of the ruling group's gods. Different empires used different strategies. In Indian kingdoms and in ancient Egypt different pantheons of gods were merged in ways that allowed specific regions, ethnic groups, or in the case of India, hereditary castes to emphasize the worship of particular members of this pantheon as long as they recognized the sacred powers of their kings. The early Roman Empire did the same, and there was a Chinese version that accepted a range of different divinities.

In what is now called the Middle East, something quite different emerged. The Jews developed the concept of a single, unique, universal God, though they maintained that they were His chosen people. This God was jealous and accepted no others, so that the Jewish Bible is full of commandments to exterminate those who threaten His primacy. In the Roman Empire, the strict, demanding Jewish God gained converts, but most of these turned to Christianity as a source of salvation in the first few centuries after the birth of Christ. In the turbulent, ethnically and religiously mixed cities of Rome the local religions of the many people who migrated into them from various provinces no longer served to meet their spiritual needs. Christianity, on the other hand, with its single God and promise of redemption from the all too real miseries of the world, did hold out such a promise. In the 4th century Rome's rulers converted to the rapidly spreading Christian faith, and saw it as a way to bind together an empire that was, by then, in danger of disintegrating. But the Christian God was also demanding. If there is but one God, there is but one true faith, and in time, those in the Empire who refused to convert came to be seen as disloyal and even dangerous outsiders. Of course, as Christianity grew, different versions and sects proliferated. After the fall of the Western Roman Empire, what remained, the Eastern Roman or Byzantine Empire was beset by a long series of religious wars between different versions of the Christian faith. Certain regions and ethnic groups used religious justifications to rebel against the center. In the West, too, the various kingdoms that succeeded Rome gradually came to impose as much religious homogeneity as possible to bolster their kings' claims to be divinely sanctioned rulers.

Within rural European communities, old practices remained alive for centuries, even until modern times, but they were covered by a general acceptance of Christianity. Yet heresies kept on coming up, often to justify regional, ethnic, or economic conflicts, and these resulted in seriously conflicting identities. Furthermore, those who did not even claim to be Christian, particularly the small, mostly urban Jewish minority, were branded as inferiors who could not be granted equal rights. This persecution of heretics and labeling of Jews as unbelievers who could not be the equal of Christians also persisted into modern times.

Islam emerged in 7th century Arabia with a heavy mixture of Judaism and Christianity, and even some elements taken from another demanding imperial religion, Persian Zoroastrianism. As another monotheistic religion, it also claimed absolute truth, and its prophet Muhammad sought to convert all of humanity. His followers conquered vast stretches of the world, and Islam came to dominate substantial portions of

Africa, Asia, and Europe. It too broke up into many conflicting sects, each of whom claimed to represent the true faith, though all recognized the sacred Quran as their holy book and Muhammad as their prophet. Muslim rulers accepted the existence of non-Muslim minorities, particularly Jews and Christians, in the lands they controlled, but these were subject to extra taxes and were legally considered inferiors.

In the parts of the world dominated by monotheism, Christian and Muslim identities became an important part of how people saw themselves, though again, this was far from being the same thing as **nationalism**. It was, however, another important way in which various groups saw themselves and distinguished themselves from non-believers. This had important political implications. When Europeans later conquered the Americas, they Christianized most of it, and when they colonized Africa they converted many there as well. Meanwhile, Islam continued to grow and spread more deeply into sub-Saharan Africa and Southeast Asia. In all these areas, especially where Christians and Muslims came to coexist in modern states, these identities are as important as ever, or perhaps even more so, and always a source of potential, or in too many cases, real conflict.

In non-monotheistic Asian cultures, various religions also became parts of people's identities, and once again, with the creation of modern states that demand greater national loyalty, the presence of mixed religious traditions has in some cases become an issue. This is particularly the case, as in Sri Lanka or some (but hardly all) parts of India, where different ethnic groups follow their own, different religious traditions.

That modern states have come into being on the ruins of religiously and ethnically mixed older agrarian kingdoms and empires has had enormous political consequences because it has created the potential for competition and conflict between different communities that identify themselves according to these older cultural traditions.

The Modern Nation-State

Today most people in the world, though not all, are members of nation-states; that is, states in which majorities owe their primary political loyalty to their states and identify with their national cultures. Most people believe they should be ruled by leaders who share their culture, their values, their language, and often, though not always, their religion. Leaders may be the descendants of **immigrants**, but they are expected to owe their loyalty to and behave like the vast majority of people they rule. And the masses are expected to share a common culture as well as to identify with the nation that dominates their states. But this is a relatively new development, so much so that most scholars who study nationalism call it a modern phenomenon. This is not strictly true, since in the past there were states, usually fairly small ones, that were more or less national, and there were certainly tribes that considered themselves to be made up of related families sharing a common culture and loyal to whatever form of government ruled them. Ancient Israel and Judea, held together by a common religion and language were something like that, as were the small, independent Greek city-states like Athens. Ancient Egypt might have been like that, too. But because the rise of complex agrarian kingdoms and empires for such a long period of time made this kind of ancient nation a fairly rare phenomenon, nationalism can be considered to be modern, and it now exists in states much larger than had been possible earlier. Nationalism claims to transcend older religious identities, though some nations claim that only one religion is genuinely national. Nationalism is supposed to supersede older ethnic, tribal, or regional identities, though some forms of nationalism also claim that only one ethnic group is fully national.

Nationalism in most of the world is the single most important political identity that people have. An American is supposed to be most loyal to and identify as a citizen of the United States rather than to her or his religion, region, or ethnicity. So it is with the French, the Japanese, Thais, Vietnamese, Tunisians, Turks, Poles, Brazilians, and so on around the world. Other identities persist, but the nation is supposed to be the supreme one.

Saying that the emphasis on unitary nationalism is relatively new, dating back at most a couple of centuries, or in some cases even less, is contentious because many, in fact most, modern nations in Europe and Asia now claim to be ancient. This is largely a myth, even though there were states ruled by elites who subsequently provided some of the cultures of modern nations. But in the agrarian past, when most people in agrarian kingdoms and empires did not participate in state politics, and were mostly illiterate, there wasn't anything like modern nationalism. People did often share a religion, as in medieval Europe, or the many Muslim kingdoms and empires, and that was an important part of their identity. But this did not necessarily endear their culturally distinct and typically rapacious rulers to them. Pre-modern agrarian states provided few services, and the people they ruled expected little of them. Modern nations are not supposed to be like that at all.

It was in the 18th century (starting earlier in a few West European cases) but very much in the 19th century that modern nationalism was created and came to dominate first Europe and then eventually the rest of the world. Today the state is supposed to provide education, jobs, economic guidance, welfare, and a vast number of other goods and services. People in these states not only expect that, but also find it normal to be mobilized by the state for wars and to produce valuable collective goods and services. In other words, in modern nations, it is not just elites who are loyal to the state and identify with it, but everyone, at least in principle. We will see that the reality is very often not quite like this.

Before getting into the anomalies that exist in many nation-states, or into the cases of states that are not inhabited by solidary nations, it is necessary to point out that even many modern nation-states are not homogeneously uni-cultural. Switzerland has four main official languages and the original Swiss were both Catholic and Protestant. There are many regional languages in Germany, and there used to be divisions between Catholics and Protestants who fought against each other in the 16th and 17th centuries. India is inhabited by people speaking many different languages and practicing many religions, and most, though not all of them, do consider themselves Indian. Immigrant nations like the United States, Argentina, Canada, Australia, Brazil, and many others are inhabited by the descendants of people who came from different cultures as well as by minorities of indigenous people whose ancestors were there to begin with. In the cases listed here, the process of nation building has succeeded pretty well, though not perfectly, and the majority of their people do identify as Americans, Argentines, Canadians, etc. Absorption of immigrants, however, has not always been smooth, and when some of these, as in the United States and Brazil, were brought over by force as slaves from Africa, **integration** with the majorities who came from Europe was neither quick nor perfectly successful.

Looked at more closely, virtually every nation has minorities because of different religions, descent from different immigrant populations, a mixing of various ethnic groups, or the persistence of strong regional feelings in states that were assembled from what were previously different political entities. This is even true in some of the nations that long considered themselves most homogeneous, such as Korea, Japan, and France.

Today, we live in an age of mass migration, and perfect cultural homogeneity is more of a myth than ever as vast numbers of migrants move from poorer to richer countries creating fears that they will dilute national cultures and endanger the nation by not being loyal. The French and most West Europeans worry about Muslim immigrants, Americans who used to worry about Irish, Italian, Slavic, and Jewish immigrants because they were not Protestant and English speaking now worry about Latin American, especially Mexican, immigrants. Thais worry about Burmese immigrants (even though they share the same kind of Buddhism) who cross the border, often illegally, to escape poverty and repression at home. This is now a global phenomenon.

This hardly means that established nation-states are disappearing. They remain the focus of political identity for most people in the world. Neither supra-national organizations like the European Union nor the growing presence of minorities in richer nation-states has lessened the power of nations to mobilize intense feelings of loyalty and a sense of belonging by the majority of their people. At the same time, there remain some states in the world that are not nations at all, and these create serious problems of their own.

States That are not Nations and Failed States

Many of today's most serious civil wars get labeled as ethnic conflicts. That is partly correct if they are between groups that identify themselves as possessing different cultural ideals. But in some of the most severe cases, what is going on is that the states in which various competing groups that identify as ethnically, religiously, linguistically, or regionally distinct are not nations at all. Some of the various groups living in these states do not identify with their governments or view them as the legitimate protectors of their lives and properties. On the contrary, they see whoever controls the machinery of their states as biased in favor of other ethnicities, religions, language groups, or regions. Sometimes this can lead to a feeling that the only solution is either for their own community to seize power, or else to secede and form their own state. Needless to say, in such conflictual situations, within any group that is angry, there are differences of opinion, and violent conflicts may well include fighting within as well as between groups and governments.

Lebanon and Afghanistan are two prominent cases. Though both have official governments and are constituted as states, neither one is a nation. Lebanon's various religious groups—many different kinds of Christians and Muslims—are almost distinct ethnic groups, and there is no majority. This is complicated by the interference of foreign states who find supporters within Lebanon, arm them, and contribute to the instability. This happens in Afghanistan, too, where state power has always been somewhat of a fiction. Local tribal, ethnic, and religious groups control their own territories, and no central government has ever exercised full control, or gained the loyalty of the entire country. And here, as in Lebanon, foreign interventions have only compounded the difficulties as they have brought in weapons from the outside and backed various factions fighting for control of the state and territory.

But these cases are hardly unique. One of the key problems faced by most, though not all, sub-Saharan African states is that they have never been and are not today nations. They were assembled into administrative units by European colonial powers who paid no attention to ethnic, tribal, or religious differences or commonalities. While most nation-states in the world came out of such circumstances, they solidified into real nations after a long period of administrative unity or cultural solidarity in which at least elites had developed a common culture and loyalty to their states. In Africa, colonialism was imposed brutally and quickly, with most boundaries hastily and arbitrarily drawn from the 1880s to early 1900s. Then, independence came very suddenly, from the late 1950s to the early 1970s, with very little preparation. Africans had been able to more or less unite in the various colonies against European rule, and this was called "nationalism," but it was not. Disliking alien, oppressive rule is one thing, but identifying with the post-colonial states that emerged was quite another. In Nigeria or the Ivory Coast, for example, tensions about who would control the state, northern Muslims or southern Christians, or which ethnic group would dominate, have never been resolved, and civil wars followed by periods of repeated ethnically and religiously motivated killings have persisted. The worst cases with the most deaths running into the many millions have been the Democratic Republic of the Congo (a **failed state** which is neither democratic nor a genuine republic) and Sudan. Hardly any independent African country has escaped such conflicts. They have been enormously aggravated by poverty, the incapacity, or sometimes unwillingness, of governments to deliver services and protection except to a favored tribe or elite, and by the intense competition for scarce goods and services that result from this. People fall back on their ethnic, religious, or linguistic group for protection because the state does not provide it, and so, naturally, they do not identify with the state as their primary political source of support.

Defining what is ethnic, religious, or linguistic can be difficult because in reality people seek to belong to an identifiable group that can protect them against others. In southern Sudan, non-Muslims who do not speak Arabic as their first language have viewed themselves as culturally distinct minorities exploited and neglected by northern Muslim Arab speakers. This was not helped by the fact that well into the 20th century northern Arabs raided the south for slaves. But within the south, different tribes who share some cultural similarities, most notably the Dinka and Nuer, have fought against each other. And in the north, Arab speakers have fought with equally Muslim non-Arabs in Darfur. All this has been for control of vital resources and power, and it is hard to say when religion has played more of a role than language differences or tribal affiliations. All of these have been in play.

In Northern Ireland, from the 1960s into the late 1990s about 3,600 people died in violence between Catholics and Protestants who speak the same language and share very similar cultural habits. This was out of a small population of only about one-and-a-half million. (If about the same percentage of people had been killed in the United States during the Civil right struggles from the 1950s to the 1980s, over a half million would have died, and the United States would be a very different kind of society.) The conflict resulted from a long period of Protestant discrimination against the Catholic minority, and that in turn was related to a much older conflict between the two sides throughout Ireland since the Protestants sided with the British when they ruled all of Ireland as a colony and treated the Catholic majority with oppressive contempt. To this day, even as peace has been more or less established between the two sides, we might as well call Northern Irish Catholics and Protestants two different ethnicities, or tribes, because the dispute between them is not really a matter of theology, and their social lives remain mostly **segregated** from each other. Whether we call the division religious or ethnic is not that important, because what really matters is that Northern Ireland is inhabited by two distinct communities whose chief loyalty and identity are based on being either Catholic or Protestant—whether one is personally religious or not.

A similar split between minority Tamils and majority Singhalese in Sri Lanka led to a 26-year civil war in which about 100,000 died. It ended with a Singhalese victory, but the issue is far from being settled. Here, there were two different ethno–linguistic–religious groups who did not form a single nation, though they are controlled by a single Singhalese-led state. The Tamils are mostly Hindu, and the Singhalese Buddhist, though there are also Christian and Muslim minorities in Sri Lanka. Again, the degree to which individuals may or may not have been religious was irrelevant compared with what community they belonged to and identified with.

A most extreme and seemingly paradoxical case of a state in Africa that fell apart because it was not a nation is Somalia, where almost all people share a common language and Muslim identity. Nevertheless, the state failed and broke apart in brutal civil war between the various clans in the early 1990s, and it has never been put back together again. Despite the absence of major ethnic, linguistic, or religious differences, the failure of nationalism and the prior existence of strong family-oriented clans led to an unending and multifaceted civil war. As broken states produce desperate **emigrants** trying to flee to other countries, havens for terrorists and pirates, and immense amounts of suffering, Somalia is more than just an odd, anachronistic anomaly; it is a major international problem.

In the part of Kashmir controlled by India, a Muslim majority would like to secede from India, and have their own nation-state. India itself is in large majority Hindu, though it has a very substantial Muslim minority. Neighboring Pakistan claims that part of Kashmir, and India will not give it up. Here we have an ethnic, regional, and religious conflict as well as an international one between India and Pakistan. Pakistan itself is in danger of disintegration as there is killing between the Shi'a Muslim minority and the Sunni Muslim majority, as well as tribal and ethno-regional conflicts that have resulted in increasing internal violence.

Whether such cases, and other similar ones, are attributed to ethnic, religious, regional, or nationalist conflicts is somewhat arbitrary and depends on one's definition of each of these terms. The essential fact is that they result from conflict between groups that identify themselves as different and struggle for the control of states and territories, and where there is no overarching nationalism to bind them together with a common political identity.

There are no Perfectly Homogenous Nation-States

If we take all the failed and semi-failed states in the world that are subject to intense clan, ethnic, tribal, religious, nationalist, and regional conflict, and we look at the international implications of these conflicts, we can easily see that these are not just minor problems that can be easily localized. Imperfectly national states are always in danger of becoming a source of violent conflict.

Given that even strongly nationalistic states also have minorities and problems dealing with them, it becomes important for us to understand how such problems have been dealt with in the past, and what can be done about them today.

DISCUSSION QUESTIONS

1. What is the most important difference in the way modern nation-states and agrarian empires and kingdoms viewed the populations they ruled?
2. Name four examples of relatively harmonious nation-states today.
3. Give two examples of failed states today.

II: Majority–Minority Problems in Modern States and Nations and Strategies for Dealing with Them

❦

There are many kinds of minority identities, even in the most solid nation-states, but most of them do not result in conflicts, and even when they do, most are not violent. But practically all modern nation-states have experienced conflicts in the past between communities of people with distinct identities of one kind or another. As we have seen, these could be ethnic, religious, regional, linguistic, tribal, or even between competing nationalities.

There have been other kinds of political conflicts, particular between different economic classes, but these have not normally threatened the unity of states, or for that matter greatly affected the rise of modern nationalism. Marxists and other kinds of socialists used to believe that class interests, specifically the antagonism between working classes and capitalist bosses could override nationalism. At the start of World War I, a conflict spawned primarily by competing nationalist claims between European nation-states, socialists hoped that working classes in Germany, France, and Great Britain would resist the siren call of nationalism and refuse to fight. But by 1914 the primary political identity of people in these highly **industrialized** societies was national, not class-related, and the industrial working classes remained loyal to their nations. This has remained true in most nation-states. Economic, that is class, identities are regularly trumped by nationalism.

That is not, however, always true of culturally and ethnically based, non-economic identities, some of which have indeed challenged nationalist unity. To understand how nationalisms in various places have succeeded in creating unity, but in other cases have failed to limit the conflict between communities within their states, it is necessary to begin by explaining why nationalism became so important in the first place in the modern world. Then we can examine strategies that have been used to overcome or render less important non-national identities and sentiments.

Why is Nationalism so Powerful?

People's group identities have always been a critically important part of how they think of themselves, something to which they turn for support, and how they explain and justify their existence. We have already seen the main kinds of group identities: Family, clan, tribe, ethnicity, community in which people live, region, or nation. Why is it that over the past two centuries the nation has become the main source of political identity for most, though not all, of the world's population?

Much of the transformation that occurred as identification with one's religion and local community and immediate region was replaced by a broader national identity was due to the economic changes that began in Western Europe in the late 1700s. Improvements in transportation, hugely accelerated with the invention of railways in the 1830s, made it far easier for people to travel away from their hometowns and villages. As industry and commerce grew, it became even more necessary for people in England, and then France and other parts of Europe, to speak a common language instead of the many regional dialects that had previously predominated. Typically, the preferred national language was that previously spoken and written by the political elite, but industrialization also meant that there was a greater need for widespread literacy, and states promoted school systems to teach the national language.

If in both England and France, the two leading European powers to develop strong nationalism, there had been dozens of local dialects that were not even mutually comprehensible, there had also long been an elite, high-culture language spoken and read by the upper classes. These elite languages had largely replaced Latin as the language of high culture and government since the invention of the printing press in the 15th century and the spread of printed books and journals in the 16th. Nascent nationalism was present, at least at the elite level, for several hundred years earlier, but it was not until the 19th century that the majority of common people learned to read and write English and French, and the same was true elsewhere in the European world, including in the United States, which began its independent existence in 1783 as the most literate of all European societies. Once literacy and newspaper reading became more widespread, and with the proliferation of schools teaching nationalist versions of history, it became possible to "nationalize," that is, turn into nationalists those masses.

Furthermore, with industrialization national economies became more integrated, and they needed workers and consumers who shared a common culture. This increased the pressure on governments to pay for school systems ranging from the lowest grades to universities, and to create opportunities for growing numbers to be educated.

That was one side of what happened. Another was that European states were in constant competition with each other. Starting with the French Revolution in 1789, first France and then its rivals got the idea of drafting huge numbers of young men to fight their wars. That the French, whose Revolution claimed to be on behalf of equality for all (which at the time meant for all men), hit on this idea first gave them a tremendous advantage as their armies conquered almost all of Europe for a brief time under Napoleon. But subsequently, all other powers caught on and did the same thing. To run a successful modern army requires that officers have technical training, and that the men under their command have a common language. The universal draft that most European states adopted (though Britain did not until much later) contributed greatly to nationalizing cultures and languages. It also contributed by making those who had served proud of their national service.

The military was not the only part of government to expand. All sorts of new services and requirements had to be established in order to maximize the nation's strength and its ability to tax the population to support growing armies and bureaucracies. There were schools to staff, censuses to conduct, roads and railways to build, police forces to create in order to keep order in the growing cities, and so on. All of these services required a common language and loyal civil servants. Also, as industrialization occurred, giant firms sprang up in key industries such as steel, railway building, and later automobiles and many others. These needed both workers and managers who understood each other and that also contributed to nationalizing the working-class masses.

Finally, nationalism enlisted the services of intellectuals—writers, artists, journalists—by creating jobs for them in government, in schools, and in subsidized institutions. Even those who did not get direct support this way relied on a growing national public to consume their products. In every state in Europe, there emerged historians who rewrote their national histories as if there had been an England, or a France, or a Germany, or Italy, or a Russia, and all the others for many centuries, or sometimes thousands of years. Much of this was mythology and hardly corresponded to what had really existed, but it was eagerly supported by governments and avidly read by the growing, literate middle classes seeking to find their identities in a changing world where old solidarities were no longer secure.

This was not just hypocritical manipulation of public opinion. Already in the late 17th and throughout the 18th centuries **Enlightenment** philosophers in Western Europe had been writing that governments owed it to those they ruled to grant greater equality and to respect the rule of law. Hereditary nobility and royalty were questioned, as was adherence to religious dogma and the arbitrary use of power by elites. Reason and science were to point the way to a better future. This was the ideology adopted by the American and French Revolutions.

From 1775 to 1783 the Americans fought their colonial masters until the British lost the war and granted the United States its independence. This resulted in the establishment of the first modern democracy guided by Enlightenment ideals that celebrated freer markets, allowed more mass participation in government, and granted individuals unprecedented personal rights that had previously only been held by elite classes. Enlightenment philosophy also urged people to stop following blind tradition just because it was there, and to think for themselves. As these ideas spread, and traditional identities were questioned, it was the nation that replaced both local and religious identities. It was the nation and its people, not the king or a hereditary aristocracy, that were now sovereign.

The later spread of nationalism outside of Europe was a direct result of the West's astounding success in using its technological and economic progress to dominate the entire globe in the 19th century. European colonization had begun much earlier, with the conquest of the Americas by the Spanish and Portuguese from the late 15th century on, and by the seizure of territories by the English, Dutch, and French starting about a century later. Outside of the Americas, the Europeans found the going much harder because in Asia local states were stronger and better able to resist, and in Africa tropical diseases, mainly malaria, kept Europeans from going inland until the late 19th century when ways were found of controlling them. Still, the Spanish, Portuguese, and subsequently the Dutch, English, and French seized trading ports and some land in South Africa (which is not tropical) and in parts of Asia. From the late 18th to the late 19th centuries, however, as the Western powers obtained ever more powerful weapons, they proceeded to conquer almost all of South and Southeast Asia, the Pacific islands, and almost all of Africa.

These colonial conquests, however, were possible for more than just the technological advantage the Westerners had in weaponry and communications technology. The enormous areas and populations they conquered were mostly still agrarian kingdoms, or in many parts of Africa clan or tribally based groups without unified states. As a result, it was relatively easy for the various European powers to use local soldiers from one ethnic or tribal group against others, and even to split up populations within existing states because there was so little sense of nationalism. There was resistance, and much fighting, but almost always factions or various communities within the conquered lands, or the existing aristocracies who had little regard for their own people, could be bribed and co-opted into cooperating with the colonizers. Where nationalism was weak or non-existent, long-term arrangements could be made that provided the colonial Westerners with native soldiers and administrators who made it possible to hold the colonies with relatively few Europeans.

The Spread of Nationalism

Nationalism first spread outside of Europe to European colonies in the Americas at the same time as it was starting to become a major force in Western Europe itself. America's native populations had been decimated by disease and brutality (they had had no immunity to the many deadly diseases Europeans, Asians, and Africans had been exposed to for thousands of years), so they were unable to mount successful resistance. But Europeans who settled in the New World came to resent being bossed around by the home countries, and first the United States, then the Latin American countries fought for and won their independence. Outside of the European settler colonies, however, it was not until later in the 19th and 20th centuries that such nationalist reactions took place.

There were differences from place to place, but many of the essentials were the same. The colonial powers needed to train local natives as administrators, and some were even sent for higher schooling to Europe itself. There they learned about modern nationalism, modern technology, and the ideals of the Enlightenment. They came back from European schools to colonies where as non-Whites they were relegated to permanent inferiority by the Europeans, and they realized that the only escape from this trap was to unite the people in their colonies against their Western masters.

Few people like to be bossed around by others, and though this had been common practice in all agrarian kingdoms and empires, the European colonizers demanded more than just basic obedience and taxes. They forced native peasants to grow cash crops for the world market or for their own Western needs. They disrupted traditional cultures and dishonored respected elders. And with only few exception, they were blatantly racist, claiming that Whites were superior while Blacks, Asians of all kinds, in fact native people everywhere were somehow "childish," "lazy," and "incapable" of running their own affairs.

In the West itself, colonialism increasingly appeared to be hugely inconsistent. The French and English, and other colonial powers (they were joined as colonial conquerors in the late 19th century by the Americans and Japanese) were intensely nationalistic at home, increasingly incorporated their masses into their political systems, and they all more or less at that time accepted many of the Enlightenment's principles. Yet in the colonies, they were not prepared to treat people as equals or give them a significant voice in governing themselves, they fought against any kind of nationalism, and they struggled to maintain what were increasingly archaic forms of governance better suited to pre-modern agrarian empires than to colonies that were being brought into the modern world economic system.

Helped by the destruction the Europeans wrought on themselves in their own nationalistic wars, World Wars I and II, the growing numbers of Westernized natives who organized their people against colonialism managed to bring down all of the European colonial empires from the late 1940s to the 1970s.

Unfortunately the collapse of empires was only the first stage in building nationalism. It was relatively easy to unite people against racist foreigners, but this all happened so quickly in many places that genuine nationalist solidarity did not extend very far once the Europeans lost power. The end of empire was the beginning of a long series of catastrophes as various ethnic, religious, and national groups in the newly liberated states began to struggle for control of governments and resources.

This brings us to the heart of the matter of why the 20th and 21st centuries have been so beset by conflicts between different groups with distinct cultural identities, some of whom claim nation status in their own right. Most, though not all, of these can be characterized as kinds of ethnic conflicts, though some of them have had a distinctly religious appearance.

The Retribalization of the Modern World and Nationalism's Troubling Excesses

As nationalism grew in Europe and began to spread elsewhere its excesses and defects as a unifying, new identity started to become more evident. For one thing, it led to intensified competition between the major European states. In the 18th century wars between the major Western powers were frequent, but tended to be limited and fought largely with mercenary, small armies. The French Revolution and Napoleon's attempts to conquer all of Europe changed that, but throughout the 19th century Europe's wars remained much more limited. By the late 19th century, however, rivalries over colonial overseas domains, greater competition within Europe itself, the far more complete mobilization made possible by the draft, and the huge leap in all technologies, including weaponry, had created giant armies capable of previously unimaginable destructive power. Backing all this was the consolidation of nationalism in all the major and many minor European powers. This eventually led to World War I, which, it should be noted, was greeted by people in the major powers, particularly France, Germany, and Russia, with enormous enthusiasm as nationalist mythologies had convinced masses of people that theirs was somehow a superior "nation" able to vanquish its enemies in short order. Instead, this turned into a long, very bloody war.

In pre-state times, tribes at war could be fully mobilized with all able-bodied men participating. Small ancient nations such as the ancient Greek city-states were able to do that as well. This had not been the case in agrarian kingdoms and especially not in the large agrarian empires, but the new nationalized states of Europe were, in a sense, retribalized on a giant modern scale.

Even before the outbreak of the great 20th century world wars, nationalism had also revealed itself to be particularly unfriendly to minorities who did not speak the national languages or share the national identities for ethnic, religious, or regional reasons. **Anti-Semitism**, long a religious prejudice throughout the Christian world, had been waning in the early 19th century, but returned in full force in the second half of that century because Jews were seen as "aliens" whose loyalties could not be counted on. Everywhere, attempts were made either to forcefully integrate minorities, or else to exclude them. This was a particularly painful process in the multi-national European empires, including Austria–Hungary, Russia, and the Ottoman Empire, where all kinds of minority ethnic groups began to demand their own independent nations. The Balkan Wars of 1912–13 in former Ottoman lands that were ethnically and religiously mixed saw episodes of mass **ethnic cleansing** and massacres that presaged what would happen in much of the rest of Europe later on, and also what happened in the Ottoman Empire where the first huge **genocide** of the 20th century took place in 1915 against the Armenians.

Nationalism also brought with it from the mid-19th century onwards new theories about why certain nations were to be considered **"races"** competing against each other for survival, and this increased racist sentiments, not only against non-Whites and against Jews, but also between competing nationalities. Germans began to think of themselves as a superior "race," as did the French, the Italians, the Russians, and others.

It would be too much here to go into the details of what happened in Europe, and how the combination of extreme nationalism, racism, and the militarization of all of its major states led finally to the rise of **fascism**, German **Nazism**, and World War II in which millions of Jews, Slavs, and Roma (often called Gypsies) were slaughtered in the name of racial purity and national glory by the Germans and their collaborators and allies throughout Europe. Over 35 million died in the war in Europe.

This went far beyond Europe, however, because Japan, the rising industrial power in Asia and that continent's most modernized nation-state adopted the same extremist ideology and launched an equally destructive, racist war in East Asia. This began with Japan's invasion of Manchuria in 1931 and eventually expanded into a huge Pacific War that killed tens of millions of Chinese and other Asians in the name of Japanese racial superiority and national glory. The United States became involved when Japan attacked it in 1941, after which the Americans also went to war against Nazi Germany. Ultimately, the Americans, the Soviet Union, the British, and their allies won World War II, but well over 50 million had died before it ended. This, too, was the product of modern nationalism.

We have seen that outside Europe colonial empires also experienced rising nationalism, at least insofar as it was directed against European colonial rule. But in the colonies, as in European states, there were mixtures of ethnic and religious groups, many languages, and different regions with their own cultures and histories. After World War II, when most colonies in Africa and Asia won their independence, practically all were faced with how to deal with their minorities and create strong nation-states.

The first major European colony to gain its independence in Asia was India, which immediately broke into two parts, Muslim Pakistan and majority Hindu India (that retained, however, a very large Muslim minority). Ethnic and religious cleansing on a huge scale led to massive population movements in northern India and the new Pakistan and to massacres that killed hundreds of thousands, perhaps over a million people in 1947–48. Many of the minority issues raised at that time remain unresolved. As in other cases, we cannot untangle whether these conflicts have been ethnic, religious, or national. All three of these identities are very closely linked for many of the people in South Asia, as elsewhere.

India was not the only case. Burma, which became independent at about the same time, almost immediately fell into civil war between competing ethnic groups, and even now, more than 60 years later, some of these wars between minority groups and the Burmese state continue.

Some colonies had to fight to gain their independence. France was defeated in Indochina, principally by the Vietnamese **Communists** who took the lead in promoting Vietnamese nationalism. The Dutch were defeated in Indonesia after a bitter war ending in 1949. France was also defeated in Algeria after another nationalist, anti-colonial war that ended in 1962. Portugal fought wars in its African possessions until forced to give up in 1974. There were other anti-colonial wars, and in some cases the British and French did better, but in the end almost all colonies gained their independence.

Nigeria, Britain's largest colony in Africa, became independent in 1960. In 1966, however, a civil war broke out as the Ibo people sought to establish their own nation in the southeast of the country. They were defeated, but only after a long and bloody war in which close to a million people died. Today strong ethnic divisions and religious differences (mostly between Muslims and Christians) continue to plague the country with thousands killed in clashes every year. The Congo gained its independence from Belgium, also in 1960, and immediately fell into a long series of ethnic and regional wars. To this day it has never been effectively reunited. Portugal's former colonies of Angola and Mozambique also slipped into ethnic civil wars after independence, as did Britain's former colony of Sudan.

Even a relatively successful African state, the Ivory Coast, split into two in 2002 in a civil war between its mostly Muslim north and its primarily Christian and animist (followers of traditional, local religions) south, largely because it failed to build a strong sense of united nationalism. When it was hit by economic problems in the 1980s and 1990s, its people turned to their ethnic, religious, and regional communities for protection rather than to a state they did not trust to defend them. This was hardly irrational as the government had been in the hands of ethnic groups from the south who had increasingly favored their own while discriminating against northerners, especially Muslims.

We will see that there are exceptions to this sad pattern in some African cases, and obviously quite a few post-colonial independent states have avoided identity-based conflicts between ethnic or other kinds of groups. But many have not.

All this historical background leads us to ask two general questions. First, what strategies have been used to try to deal with minorities in nationalizing states? Second, why has the nationalizing project worked in some cases, but not in others, and what role do various kinds of non-national identities play in hindering or helping the construction of nationalist solidarities?

The Various Ways of Dealing with Minorities as Part of Nation Building

Not all majority–minority ethnic, religious, or national identities are conflictual. Sometimes, as we have seen in cases such as Switzerland's, different language groups and religions can coexist peacefully and even share a common national identity. In Canada, though there have been movements to separate French-speaking Quebec and make it an independent state, very little violence was involved, and now it seems that French and English speakers exist together as Canadians, along with the descendants of many indigenous communities. In India, despite the existence of several ethnic, religious, and regional conflicts, most of the large number of linguistic and religious communities have peaceful relations and over time have come to consider themselves loyal Indian nationalists. The many different languages in China have not prevented the consolidation of a very strong Chinese national identity among the Han people who make up over 90 percent of China's population, though that is not the case with some non-Han minorities, particularly Tibetans and Muslims Uighurs. It would be possible to list many hundreds of cases of how various cultural identities have come to co-exist and accept certain strong national loyalties. Of course, there are many cases where this has not happened. Much depends on strategies used to incorporate different communities in the process of nation building.

There are tolerant and intolerant approaches, and three different basic strategies: inclusion, separation that emphasizes irresolvable distinctions, and exclusion. As these three may be divided into tolerant and intolerant approaches, this makes six kinds of strategies. Table 2.1 summarizes these.

The United States, a very important case of a nation composed of many different ethnicities, religions, and regions has at one time or another practiced all of these in dealing with various minorities. Originally the American national identity was based on an adaptation of British Protestant culture, though from the start other religions were tolerated. Gentle **assimilation** became the preferred and most common strategy used with waves of subsequent, non-British immigrants from Europe. Though for a long time there were prejudices against new arrivals, especially if they were not northern Europeans, the United States allowed ethnic groups of immigrants to have their own associations, churches, newspapers, and even political movements. The understanding was that eventually immigrants, or at least their children, would become English-speaking Americans whose primary political identity and loyalty would be to the American nation. By and large, that is what happened to Irish, Italian, German, Scandinavian, Jewish, Russian, and other immigrants. Separate identities remained and people could identify themselves as "Irish-American" or other kinds of so-called "hyphenated Americans," but the assumption was and remains that all of them are more American than anything else.

That, however, was not the entire picture. There was always a great deal of intolerance. The most egregious cases were based on what Americans called race, a term that in the United States refers to skin color. Native Americans were in some cases slated for extermination, or if they were not killed, they were herded into restrictive reservations after their lands had been taken from them.

Table 2.1 Strategies for Dealing with Minorities within the State

	Inclusion	Separation/Distinction	Exclusion
Tolerant	Gentle assimilation	Multiculturalism	Voluntary separation or emigration
Intolerant	Forced assimilation	Segregation	Ethnic cleansing or genocide

Black African slaves were brought to the United States (starting well before it became independent) and eventually formed a significant portion of the population. As slaves, African-Americans were considered racial inferiors who could never be assimilated. Slavery was in complete contradiction to the Enlightenment principles on which the United States was based, that "all men are created equal." In the American South, where slavery was a very important part of the plantation economy that produced major cash crops, chiefly cotton, a whole ideology developed that claimed that Africans were not quite human, so this principle did not apply. Even in the American North, as anti-slavery sentiment grew, there was a feeling that Whites and Blacks could never be on an equal footing. Still, most Northerners came to feel that slavery was inherently evil, and that Blacks were, after all, human beings.

Most Americans know, but have tended to overlook the fact, that the South and the North developed such different cultures, ideologies, and political sentiments that by the time the Civil War broke out in 1860 over the question of slavery, these were for practical purposes two different nations. That is exactly what the Southern Confederacy tried to create—its own nation-state. At tremendous cost in America's bloodiest war (600,000 died), the Confederacy was defeated and the slaves were freed. But this did not end the feeling of Southerners that they were different. Eventually, a bargain was struck between the North and the South to bind the nation back together again. The South was allowed through **segregation** and a whole set of discriminatory laws to make African-Americans an underclass with few opportunities for education or advancement, and with no political rights. They were bound to the land by debt and restrictive laws, so that something analogous to slavery was recreated. Over time, White Southerners accepted being American, but the North had reincorporated them into the nation by abandoning the rights of the Black population for another century after the Civil War. It was not until the 1960s that legal segregation began to end. So, for a long time, the strategy toward African-Americans was based on the notion that they were too distinctive, that is too inferior, to be treated in the same way as Americans descended from European immigrants. This fit into the category of "intolerant separation." African-Americans were American, English speaking Christians, but they were kept segregated from the White majority, either by law in the southern United States or by custom in other parts.

Some anti-slavery Whites before the Civil War, including President James Monroe and for a time Abraham Lincoln, also believed that Blacks could never really be assimilated into American life, and so should be freed but then encouraged to move back to Africa. In 1847 Liberia in West Africa was set up as an independent state by freed American slaves who named their capital Monrovia. This was a kind of tolerant exclusion—get Blacks to leave, but as free people who were supposed to set up their own new nation. Lincoln and others eventually recognized that this was not practical as the huge majority of freed slaves were no longer African and had no wish to emigrate.

Native Americans who were not killed were at first segregated into reservations, but schools were set up for them that attempted to force them to become English speakers and adopt "American ways." Canadians did the same with many of their indigenous people. This amounted to what can be called forced assimilation. In Australia the authorities went so far as to forcibly remove some, particularly mixed-race Aborigines (their term for the indigenous population), from their families.

But in the United States, as in some Latin American colonies, and with many Aboriginal tribes in Australia, intolerance went beyond forced assimilation or segregation into special reserves. Whole groups were wiped out in what amounted to genocidal campaigns. This was "intolerant exclusion," that is, a strategy based on the notion that they could never be assimilated, that they were in the way of European settlers, and therefore they were condemned to death.

Some groups of immigrants to the United States have for long periods of time been treated intolerantly. As European immigrants were being gradually assimilated, for decades there were laws prohibiting Asian ones from being treated equally, though that is no longer the case, and descendants of Japanese immigrants are now among the most assimilated of immigrant groups in the United States because so many have married non-Japanese. In more recent years, immigrants from Vietnam, and increasingly from India have been assimilating, but problems remain in assimilating immigrants from Latin America, and there are political pressures to exclude many of them.

Most recently, **multiculturalism**, or the tolerant recognition of lasting differences between various ethnic groups, has been advocated in the United States. Compared with the genuine multiculturalism that exists in India with its many languages and regions, or even in Canada with two official languages, Americans tend to mean something rather different, namely that assimilation should be gradual and tolerant, and that existing cultural differences between various groups ought not be a reason to worry about any community's loyalty toward the United States. Perhaps the ultimate test will come with respect to the assimilation of Muslim immigrants who some see as threatening to place their religious identity above being American.

In Western Europe where there are now many more Muslim immigrants, that has become one of the most burning political issues, as some Europeans maintain that Islam makes it impossible for these immigrants to ever become "really" French, Dutch, British, German, or any other kind of European. Some of the remedies being proposed include forced assimilation or exclusion, while others propose either tolerant assimilation or multicultural solutions.

Looking around the world, examples of all of the possible strategies for dealing with minorities can be found. Gentle assimilation exists in many places, and in fact occurred at some time in the past in almost all nations as local dialects and habits were blended into a national identity.

Multiculturalism, that is the recognition of continuing differences and the practice of allowing communities to remain distinct within the nation, has worked occasionally, but has also frequently failed. This was the idea behind the way Lebanon was set up as an independent state, with distinct political positions reserved for Christians, Sunni Muslims, and Shiite Muslims. But Lebanon proved to be too complex, with some excluded communities like the Druzes (an offshoot of Islam that has become its own ethnic community) unhappy with this arrangement. In the 1980s Lebanese multiculturalism broke down into bitter civil war between the many groups, a situation that remains unresolved. Another case of failed multiculturalism is Belgium where Dutch-speaking Flemish people and French-speaking Walloons cannot get along, and their disputes have paralyzed the Belgian state. There is no violence, but no agreement to be loyal to a common nation either.

One of the most dramatic cases of failed multiculturalism occurred in Yugoslavia where each of the main ethno-religious communities was supposed to have a considerable degree of political autonomy. Yugoslavia was composed of mostly Catholic Slovenes and Croats, mostly Eastern Orthodox Christian Serbs, Montenegrins, and Macedonians, and mostly Muslim Albanians and Bosnians. There was also a Hungarian minority, and small numbers of others. All this was pieced together after World War I, but it never worked very well, largely because Slovenes and Croats were more Westernized and richer, and they resented being dominated by the more numerous but less economically advanced Serbs. During World War II, the Germans and Italians occupied Yugoslavia, and encouraged an ultra-nationalist Croatian Fascist party to start massacring Serbs as well as members of the small Jewish community. There resulted a bitter civil war that was ended by a Communist victory in 1945 and the imposition of a dictatorship that then held the country together into the 1980s. But again, Slovenes and Croats resented having to subsidize the poorer other regions, and Serbs were angered by the autonomy of Kosovo that was dominated by Albanian-speaking Muslims. After Yugoslavia's Communist dictator Tito died in 1980, the government was paralyzed by endless disputes between these communities. This was aggravated by economic troubles and inflation, and in 1991 the country split apart. Unfortunately, by that time populations were very mixed, and there resulted horrible episodes of ethnic cleansing and genocidal massacres, as each region's majority attempted to purify its territory of the various minorities in order to create homogeneous new nation-states. Ultimately, hundreds of thousands were killed and over a million people displaced. Today most of the seven republics that emerged from this mess are indeed more homogeneous, but this was achieved at tremendous cost, and some of these new states remain hopelessly dysfunctional.

What happened in Yugoslavia in the 1990s was actually the last act of a long process of intolerant exclusion that occurred in most of the nations that emerged from the fallen Austro-Hungarian and Ottoman Empires in the late 19th century and after World War I. All had mixed populations and severe minority problems, but through wars, expulsions, and massacres, they have all become more homogeneous nations. The new Polish state after World War I was 10 percent Jewish, and another quarter of its population was not Polish Catholic. Ninety percent of the Jews were slaughtered by the Nazis during World War II, Poland's borders were forcefully shifted westward so that most of the Ukrainian and Byelorussian population were excluded, the German minority was expelled after the war, and the remaining Jews were forced to flee. Today Poland is a culturally much more homogeneous, intensely nationalistic and Catholic state. Large Jewish communities in Romania and Hungary also were wiped out by the war, thus solving their so-called "Jewish problem." Hungarian minorities that remained in neighboring states were politically marginalized. Earlier, in the 1920s, Greece and Turkey engaged in massive ethnic cleansing and expulsions as substantial Muslim minorities were forced to leave Greece, and Christians were expelled from Turkey or killed.

Though many factors can explain why there was so much violence in Central and Eastern Europe, the most important cause was the intense and intolerant nationalism that swept through Europe in the late 19th and early 20th centuries, and remains a strong force to this day, even though by now there has been enough "intolerant exclusion" to make these passions less deadly. Nations have fewer minorities to worry about, but this has happened only after 80 years of tragedy.

Czechoslovakia, once part of the Austro-Hungarian Empire, also became independent in 1918 after World War I. It included a problematic large German minority that was not loyal to the state. This minority of some three million joined with Nazi Germany to destroy the Czechoslovak state at the start of World War II. The rationale was that all German speakers deserved to be part of Germany, and not have to be subjected to rule by others. But when Germany lost the war, these Czech Germans were forcibly deported, thus ending that particular ethnic problem.

More recently, however, Czechoslovakia has shown that exclusion can take a different form. Even after the expulsion of the German minority, there remained antagonism between equally Catholic Czechs and Slovaks. As in Yugoslavia they were held together by a Communist dictatorship until 1989 when communism collapsed. But instead of following the Yugoslav path, Czechs and Slovaks resolved their differences peacefully in 1993 when the two amicably split into two different nation-states. This fit into the category of "tolerant exclusion." To be able to separate like that requires both sides to agree on borders and the division of assets, and this can be done, but it is relatively rare, as most states are unwilling to give up territory.

There have been other cases of national division between ethnic, linguistic, or religious communities who have been unable to agree on how to form a single nation, but most of these have been bloody. We have looked at the case of the India–Pakistan split. In Africa, Eritrea fought a long, destructive war against Ethiopia to gain its separate independence, and after that happened, there was another war between the two who remain enemies. Cyprus became independent in 1960 (it had been part of the Ottoman Empire, and then a British colony) with a Greek Christian majority and a Turkish Muslim minority. The majority did not grant the Turks equal rights, and after a simmering conflict that erupted into serious violence in 1974, Turkey invaded the north of the island. There followed massive ethnic cleansing, with Turks settling in the north, and Greeks in the south, whereas before the populations had been quite mixed. The situation remains unsolved, with the island divided into two parts. Whereas a policy of genuine multiculturalism might have worked, the Greek majority opted for an intolerant version of discriminating against Muslim Cypriots, and the result was a disaster.

Unfortunately, similar situations exist in many other cases where majorities have chosen to impose their will on minorities and given them the choice of either changing their identities completely, or being marginalized. Particularly where minorities are actually majorities in a particular region, or where the differences between them and the majority can only be erased very gradually, over centuries, as between Christians and Muslims, the potential for civil war and bitter conflict is high. Muslims in majority Buddhist Thailand, for example, have felt marginalized, and there is chronic violence, though no all-out civil war. Tribal minorities in Pakistan have never accepted central rule, and their primary political allegiance is not to the Pakistani nation but to their tribes. This also has resulted in chronic violence. Equally Muslim East and West Pakistan were united after independence in a single state, but the cultures and languages of both parts were very different, and this eventually produced a deadly civil war in which hundreds of thousands, some say millions, were killed. The war ended in 1971 when East Pakistan became the new nation-state of Bangladesh.

Political differences between poor rural areas and the dominant political elite in Guatemala were exacerbated by the fact that the descendants of indigenous Maya people were predominantly poor and felt exploited by the higher-status descendants of European, mostly Spanish, immigrants, and this resulted in a civil war in the 1970s and 1980s in which an estimated 200,000, mostly Maya, people were killed. We could go on to name many more cases.

All this is not to say that wherever there are ethnic or other identity differences there is necessarily violence. Most of the time, even in cases that have erupted in conflict, there have been periods of peaceful relations between groups. But if intolerant strategies are practiced to strengthen national identities, communities that feel persecuted, or are left out, will harbor resentment, and in moments of economic or political crisis there is a high likelihood that violence will erupt.

DISCUSSION QUESTIONS

1. Why is nationalism such a powerful political force in the modern world?
2. How did nationalism spread far beyond where it originated in Europe?
3. What are the six possible strategies for dealing with minority ethnic or religious groups in modern nation-states?

III: War or Peace?

The Range of Possible Ethnic and Other Identity Conflicts

~~~⚬×~~~

There exist many different kinds of identity conflicts within states striving to be nations. These range from very mild differences between regions, language groups, or religions that do not result in conflicts within modern nations all the way to conflicting identities so strong and irreconcilable that they end up with civil war or even ethnic cleansing and genocide. The possible outcomes with some illustrative examples are summarized in Table 3.1 (parts A through F). Examples are from the 20th and 21st centuries.

Not included in the tables will be cases of sub-national identities so weak that the issue of possible conflict does not even come up. There are thousands of examples. For example, Burgundians in France do not claim a potentially disruptive identity even though in the 15th century there was once a separate Burgundian state. Americans in Oregon and Ohio in the United States do not see themselves as being in a conflictual situation with their American identity even though Oregon and Ohio have their own "state" governments. (American states are not sovereign states at all but are what otherwise would be called provinces of the national state.) People from Shanghai who have a distinct regional dialect are no less Han Chinese for that. But why in some cases do such differences turn into serious identity conflicts, while in other cases they remain mild regional identities that have no chance of leading to serious conflict? In going through Tables 3.1 and 3.2 and the explanations that follow we will find some answers.

Before explaining Table 3.1A through F in more detail and seeing how conflicts can move up or down in their level of violence, it is important to point out that at least categories B, C, D, and E end up being resolved and followed by peace. Three kinds of resolution are possible, as shown in Table 3.2. In a sense, if genocide or thorough ethnic cleansing takes place, as in category F, that also resolves the issue, though most of us would not call that a genuine "resolution."

Though the examples provided in Tables 3.1 and 3.2 are far from exhaustive because many other cases could be put into each category, they are illustrative and important cases. Each case has its own unique characteristics, but we need to ask what they may have in common, and most crucially, why do some cases turn into ever more serious violent confrontation and war, while others never develop that far, and some move in the opposite direction, from violence to peace?

Table 3.1 Levels of Ethnic, Religious, or Regional Conflict

(A) Very Low Levels of Ethnic, Religious, or Regional Conflict

Low Level of Conflict	Cases	Remarks
No serious conflict despite high-level awareness about and important political role of ethnic, regional, and/or religious differences.	Switzerland (different languages and religions); Germany (different German languages, religions); Tanzania (excluding Zanzibar—dozens of different tribal identities); Burkina Faso (several major linguistic and ethnic groups); Belize (Afro-Caribbean, Maya, and Spanish-speaking cultures); Finland (Swedish minority); Singapore (Chinese majority with Malay Muslim and Indian minorities); New Zealand (Europeans and Maori—but earlier there was violent conflict); China (Han areas only—many different languages and regional identities).	There are many examples, but some of them could change and become sources of conflict, others not. Some American "states," called provinces in other countries, for example Texas, have such strong political identities that they might fit into this category. The same can be said about some ethnic groups in the United States.

(B) Political Ethnic, Religious, or Regional Conflicts without Violence

Some Political Conflict but without Violence	Cases	Remarks
Fairly serious political conflict, but without systemic violence, though there may be some sporadic occasions when it does occur.	Belgium (French and Dutch speakers); Estonia (large Russian minority); Malaysia (Malay majority with large Chinese and Indian minorities); Latvia (large Russian minority); Guyana (Afro-Caribbeans and descendants of migrants from India with a small indigenous minority); Canada (English-speaking majority with large French minority and many indigenous groups); Slovakia (significant Hungarian minority); Spain (except for Basque region where there is some violence—strong Catalonian autonomy and some other—particularly Galician—regional identities).	Also very common. Today many West European states have large Muslim immigrant minorities, and this is causing increasingly contentious political issues, but so far there has been only sporadic violence. At times political interactions between various ethnic groups in the United States might fit into this category, particularly Black–White relations.

(C) Ethnic, Religious, or Regional Conflict with Fairly Frequent Violence but No War

Conflict with Sporadic Violence but no War	Cases	Remarks
Conflict, not all-out war, but some serious violence, either endemic or at least repetitive and expected.	United States into the 1960s (there were regular episodes of lynching and race riots in the United States, but such violence is now rare); Nigeria (violent ethnic conflict in the Niger River Delta and killings between Christians and Muslims); Indonesia (several regions had violent ethnic conflicts in the recent past, but now this is confined mostly to West Irian where there is a kind of civil war, but until not long ago there was civil war in Aceh where Acehnese nationalists called for independence, and earlier a bloody war in which East Timor gained its independence	Conflicts here can move either up or down in severity. The United States is now mostly at level B or perhaps even A where there is a high level of awareness that various ethnic communities are politically at odds with each other, but where there is little violence. In Nigeria there was a major ethnic war in the 1960s, and some would characterize the present situation in the Niger Delta as a near war.

in 2002); Egypt (repeated incidents of violence against Christian minority); Northern Ireland (before 1998 there was something close to a civil war between Catholics and Protestants, but now violence has become rare); China (non-Han areas, particularly Tibet and Xinjiang where a large Uighur minority resides); many parts of India (in Kashmir, however, there is a low-level war); Rwanda (now violence is sporadic, but in 1994 it was extreme and genocidal).

(D) Ethnic, Religious, or Regional Conflict That Result in Low-Level War and may be between Competing Nationalities

Low-Level War	Cases	Remarks
Conflict, low-level war over control of the state or possible demands for separation over competing nationalist claims.	Israel/Palestine (Israel is strong enough to control the Palestinian Arabs in the West Bank, to repress Gaza, and to dominate Arabs within Israel proper, but it is only repression that has kept full-scale war from breaking out the way it has with Israel's Arab neighbors); South Africa, until 1990 (the African National Congress waged a low-level war against White rule, and eventually won, so that South Africa today is somewhere between categories B and C); Burma (in some ethnic rebellious regions there is low-level war, but in others larger-scale war); Philippines (Muslim south); Kashmir (Muslim majority unhappy about being in India); Senegal (Casamance region where population is ethnically different from the majority, and also not highly Muslim, as are the majority of other Senegalese).	Some of these situations are very unstable and can easily plunge into major wars resulting in either massive repression or the establishment of breakaway new states, as happened with East Timor's long war fought against Indonesia's 1975 annexation. Others, however, can result in peaceful resolution, as has happened in South Africa.

(E) Major Wars over Conflicting Ethnic, Religious, Regional, or Nationalist Claims

Major War	Cases	Remarks
War with high rates of killing and possible large-scale forced migrations, but not genocide.	Sri Lanka until 2009 (between minority Tamils and majority Singhalese); Iraq (bloody civil war after the American invasion, mostly between Sunni and Shiite Muslims Arabs but also between Kurds and Arabs at a less intense level, and also growing incidence of Muslims killing members of the Christian minority); Yugoslavia in the 1990s; Turkey's Kurdish War until 1999 (though now it continues at a less intense level); Guatemala in the 1970s/80s (a mostly political war that took on an ethnic element as the	Many cases can alternate between categories D and E, like Chechnya. Guatemala's wasn't a purely ethnic war, but ethnic differences played a role. In many cases as in Chechnya or Yugoslavia it is difficult to distinguish between ethnic and religious war as ethnic identities are closely correlated with religious ones. (*continued*)

Table 3.1 Continued

(E) Major Wars over Conflicting Ethnic, Religious, Regional, or Nationalist Claims (*continued*)

indigenous Maya population was the most targeted for killing); Russia (long wars waged by Muslim Chechen insurgents against Russia, with low-level violence spreading to other Muslim areas in Russia's North Caucasus region).

(F) Genocides and Similar Large-Scale Exterminations of Groups Based on their Ethnicity or Religion		
Genocide or Large-Scale Extermination	Cases	Remarks
Genocide or large-scale, deliberate extermination campaigns. These may start as or be justified as large-scale ethnic cleansing but result in a very high proportion of deaths.	Herero 1904/5 (German colonizers get revenge for uprising by Africans in Southwest Africa—today's Namibia); Armenians 1915 (attempt by Ottomans to ethnically cleanse large parts of Anatolia); Jews 1939–45 (Nazi Germany's attempt to destroy all of Europe's Jews); Cambodia 1975–79 (Khmer Rouge slaughter of one-quarter of their population, but this was only partially ethnic—against Vietnamese and Cham minorities—and more largely based on economic class and region in which people lived); Rwanda 1994 (attempt by Hutu political elite to kill all Tutsis and opposition Hutus); Darfur until recently (Sudanese Arab elite's attempt to ethnically cleanse Darfur region of opposition ethnic groups). Many would call the Indonesia war against East Timor's liberation movement genocidal as one-third of East Timor's population died in the war that followed Indonesia's annexation of the region in 1975.	These are rare, but kill many. Using the term "genocide" is contentious. Sudan has been at level E most of the time since it became independent in 1956. Chapter V in this book will be devoted to explaining genocide.

Table 3.2 Resolution of Identity Conflicts

(A) Peaceful Resolution		
Accommodation	Cases	Remarks
Past violent conflicts followed by reconciliation or accommodation (no partition).	South Africa (apartheid ends and free elections in 1994 bring the African Black majority to power); Northern Ireland (agreements in 1998 to share power between Catholics and Protestants greatly diminish violence, which is now rare); Malaysia (ethnic riots and killings in 1969 not repeated as Malays continue to dominate the political system, but Chinese and Indian minorities retain most of their rights, and the Chinese in particular prosper); U.S. South (civil rights legislation	Civil wars ended or averted despite lasting bitter memories and fear that some of these situations might again resurface. In the United States, the North–South conflict over slavery from 1860 to 1865 was extremely bloody, and it took over a century for the ensuing racial problems to move toward some sort of acceptable resolution.

and integration forced on the South by the dominant North gradually take hold and are now widely, though not totally, accepted by Whites); Indonesia (Aceh's war of independence was resolved peacefully in 2005, as are most other prior regional uprisings and local wars, though a low-level war persists in West Irian, and East Timor is an exception as it split off from Indonesia in 2002).

(B) Partition

Creation of New and Separate Nations	Cases	Remarks
Past conflicts followed by partition, sometimes quite amicable, sometimes not at all.	Sweden–Norway (1905 split without war); Czechoslovakia (1993 split without war); Cyprus (1974 partition after Turkish invasion of the north, a situation that remains unresolved though there is no fighting); Ethiopia–Eritrea (1993 split after a long war of independence, though relations between the two remain very unfriendly); Ireland–United Kingdom (1922 split after Ireland wins its violent war of independence against Britain, though the Northern Ireland problem remained a British-ruled problem for a long time).	The division of Cyprus is not internationally recognized, though it has brought peace to the island. Nationalist grievances can easily produce civil war but can also be resolved peacefully.

(C) Suppression

Violent Control of Protest	Cases	Remarks
One side wins or has sufficient power to repress most protest and violence.	Sri Lanka (2009 the Singhalese majority defeats a long-standing Tamil rebellion in a very bloody war); China in Tibet (China has repeatedly crushed any potential uprising or protest); USSR (when Russia was the larger Soviet Union, it violently crushed a number of regional nationalist movements, though after the Soviet Union collapsed in 1991 Russia was unable to hold on to the non-Russian provinces that split off peacefully and became 14 independent new states); Indonesia in West Irian where a low-level war continues but looks increasingly hopeless).	This rarely ends the problem. Though it may suppress it for a long time, it leaves lasting hostility between minorities and the dominant state. Israel's control of Palestinians is an illustrative case.

DISCUSSION QUESTIONS

1. Give at least two major examples of:
    a. states where people are highly aware of ethnic, regional, and religious differences, but these do not produce serious conflicts;
    b. states where such differences are an important source of political disputes, but these do not produce violence;
    c. states where such differences are the cause of frequent violence;
    d. cases where the conflicts that result from such differences have led or still lead to low-level warfare;
    e. cases where such conflicts have led to serious civil war;
    f. cases of genocide in the 20th or 21st centuries.
2. What are the three main ways in which serious ethnic, religious, or regional conflicts that have led to violence can be resolved?

IV: Causes of Increasing or Decreasing Conflicts

❧

There are many possible kinds of political identity that bind groups of people together into communities able to act together in order to defend and further their interests, but many of these are not activated, and even the most important ones come into play only from time to time. We have seen that many potential ethnic and regional identities never turn into meaningful political ones. Others may have been important in the past but no longer are. The same is true for religions. While people do not simply shed their religions, their beliefs do not necessarily become politically relevant. The same even holds true for nationalism. While strong nationalism can produce intense emotions and even a willingness to die for one's nation, that is hardly on most people's minds except during unusual times. Usually nationalist feelings remain in the background. In other words, all of these potential sources of community solidarity and action are contingent. Only certain kinds of situations turn them into powerful political forces.

Real or Imagined Threats

A perceived threat against one's nation, ethnicity, religion, or even one's local community, is likely to strengthen internal bonds and awaken solidarity. After the attack on Pearl Harbor by the Japanese on December 7, 1941, a previously deeply divided American public rallied to the cause of war in a wave of patriotic unity. The same happened after the destruction of the World Trade Center in New York on September 11, 2001.

The same can occur if a particular ethnic or religious group within a nation or state feels attacked. This is why politicians labeled "ethnic entrepreneurs" will try to mobilize support by claiming, rightly or wrongly, that their community is under attack. (Remember that a religious community can behave like, and be perceived in the same way as, an ethnic one.) After the death of Hindu pilgrims in what was almost certainly a train accident, Hindu extremist politicians in the Indian province of Gujarat claimed this was part of an attack on their religion by Muslims, and provoked a massacre of some two thousand Muslims. This was part of a general strategy by an extremist political party to mobilize majority Hindu opinion for itself. The central government of India, which does not sanction religious extremism, had to intervene to stop the killing.

At a more global level, attacks against Muslims anywhere in the world, or even the spread of fabricated rumors of such attacks, serve as a way for Muslim extremists to recruit converts ready to lay down their lives in holy war to defend their faith. Publicizing, exaggerating, or fabricating such incidents is an important tool used by extremist leaders to win converts.

In general, any communal identity will find potential leaders who will try to create a perception of threat and persecution in order to gain followers. Clearly, the more real the threat, the more likely it is that the appeal will have some success. But sometimes, the mere successful resurrection of memories of past persecutions can have the same effect, especially if it is combined with persuasive claims that the same thing is about to happen again, or outraged claims that past persecutions have remained unpunished. This is what happened in Yugoslavia in the 1980s and 1990s when Serbian leader Slobodan Milosevic appealed to historical injustices against Serbs (some of which were based on ancient myths) to intensify resentment and fears of future persecution and mobilize Serbian nationalism. This played directly into the hands of Croatian, Slovenian, Bosnian Muslim, and Albanian Muslim nationalists who energized their own communities by citing the Serbian threat. Since the Yugoslav economy was already in trouble, and the central government was paralyzed, the panic of each ethnic community was sharpened by fears that if they remained in a Serbian-dominated Yugoslavia they would suffer. The result was a terrible civil war.

The same had happened in the 19th century in the United States as Southern, pro-slavery leaders, fearing correctly that the institution of slavery was under grave attack, mobilized their people, pushed regional resentment and nationalism, and tried to create a whole new nation-state in 1860.

Discrimination

The civil war in Sri Lanka from 1983 to 2009 was the result of years of systematic official prejudice against mostly Hindu Tamils who were denied their share of good jobs and educational opportunities by the majority Buddhist Singhalese. After roughly 100,000 deaths, mostly in the north where Tamils predominate, the rebellion was finally crushed; but the problem is unlikely to end as the winning majority shows few signs of being willing to change its ways. This conflict illustrates the fact that when ethnic, regional, and religious identities are highly correlated, and a particular minority community feels discriminated against but is a majority in a particular region, the likelihood of separatist conflict is high. This is the case in Indian Kashmir where a long-running, low-level civil war is fed by the region's Muslim majority's discontent. A similar problem is developing in the

Muslim Malay-speaking part of southern Thailand. Thailand's majority population speaks Thai and is Buddhist.

Governments that favor a particular clan, region, ethnic, or religious group, leaving others discontented and increasingly frustrated, cause many African civil wars. In South Africa, it was minority Whites who segregated, demeaned, and denied opportunities to Blacks. In other cases, ranging from the Ivory Coast to Rwanda to Somalia and Angola, clan, tribal, and regional favoritism sparked uprisings and widespread killings. Again, leaders of groups engaged in conflicts promoted differences by emphasizing the threats to their communities, but in the absence of real grievances, such appeals would have been unlikely to create so much violence.

Economics: Security or Crisis?

In most of Africa, widespread failure to achieve satisfactory economic growth has made ethnic divisions much worse. In a situation where there are few or decreasing benefits to hand out, the state and its government are less likely to try to lessen tensions by giving in to demands for more benefits. Absolute poverty is not necessary, since, for example, in the case of Yugoslavia only a relative economic decline contributed to the collapse. In absolute terms, Yugoslavia was still much richer than many stable countries in other parts of the world. The combination of existing strong ethnic or other similar political identities, a legacy of past wrongs, incendiary leaders, and a perception of economic crisis is likely to lead to violent conflict, especially if aggrieved minorities are concentrated in a particular region. As we have seen above, in less dire economic conditions, and in a situation where there was less of a legacy of 20th century deadly conflict, Czechoslovakia split into two nation-states in 1993 with no violence at all.

To resolve such situations peacefully requires the availability of resources to satisfy at least some of the demands of angered communities, leaders willing to compromise, and the calming of fears on all sides. Thus, for example, French-speaking Quebec was soothed by Canada's willingness to give in to many of its leaders' demands short of full independence, but this was far easier in an economically secure situation than if English and French speakers had been involved in a desperate struggle for declining resources. Then, also, some key leaders, particularly Prime Minister Pierre Trudeau, who was perfectly bilingual, eased tensions by being conciliatory.

A more dramatic case was in South Africa. Whites gave in to the African National Congress's (ANC) demands after a long struggle, but they were promised that their property would not be threatened, and that no retaliatory measures would be taken against them. A key was that the leader of the Whites in the late 1980s and early 1990s, F. W. de Klerk, was willing to compromise to escape South Africa's increasing isolation, though some in his party wanted to fight to the bitter end. Even more importantly, the ANC leader, Nelson Mandela, called for moderation even though he had been imprisoned for much of his adult life. He suppressed his bitterness and anger at the injustices his people has suffered and did not demand revenge or the confiscation of White property, as some of his followers wanted. But if South Africa had not had Africa's strongest economic base from which to start, if there had been no reasonable (and as yet not really fulfilled) promise that there was prosperity to be shared, it is unlikely that his appeals for moderation would have been heeded, and an all-out White–Black war would probably have ensued, with catastrophic consequences for all concerned.

In the United States, there were several reasons why the civil rights struggle to emancipate Blacks from segregation and injustice succeeded with relatively little violence. There was some violence, but it pales in comparison to what has happened in the many other ethnic conflicts we have listed. An important reason was that the key Black leader, Martin Luther King, called for peaceful, not violent, protest. Not all Blacks agreed, but most went along. On the other side, the powers of the American Government eventually took the side of emancipation and justice. There were, to be sure, Southern leaders who said their culture and way of life were threatened, and they promised to fight back. In the end, however, there was no threat of confiscation of property, no economic reprisals against the South, and in an age of great American prosperity, reform was easier than if there had been an economic crisis. Nor should we forget that Martin Luther King was a Protestant Christian minister whose religion was in many ways similar to that of Southern Whites and the majority of Americans, something that made it harder to reject his claims for equality.

One of the reasons Malaysia has escaped violent ethnic conflict between its large ethnic mostly Buddhist Chinese minority and its mostly Muslim Malay majority is that even though the Chinese have been somewhat discriminated against, as a whole they have been allowed to prosper and to participate in government. The tremendous economic growth experienced from the 1970s to 2000s made compromise easier. Ethnic tensions remain, but Malaysia has not suffered from ethnic violence in the past four decades.

All complex modern societies have richer and poorer regions, and some ethnic or religious groups are more economically successful, either because they are favored by the state, or because of some cultural and historical advantages that have better prepared them to deal with modern economies. Chinese in Southeast Asia, for example in Malaysia, have long been, on average, more economically successful than Malays, and this was a major source of tension that Malaysia has tried to remedy by favoring Malay entrepreneurs. There are many similar cases, some of which have been successfully resolved, and others not. Economic inequalities are a frequent source of conflict, but they are hardly the only, or sometimes not even the main cause of ethnic, religious, and regional conflicts.

Just as it takes a number of factors in combination to aggravate communal conflicts, it also requires several to do the opposite and ease tensions. Skillful moderate leadership and urging people not to demand revenge for past injustices are important. But easing economic fears is also essential.

State Failure as a Major Cause of Conflict

A state's success or failure in making economic progress and delivering services can make an enormous difference in either creating a unifying nationalism able to surmount ethnic, religious, regional, and tribal differences, or conversely, in producing increasing communal conflicts. Pakistan, since its independence in 1947, has consistently failed to provide the kinds of economic and social progress required to consolidate its national unity. One reason has been that a fairly small elite has kept too much control over the economy, including land, and too much attention has been paid to pursuing a hostile relationship with neighboring India. Combined with many years of military rule, this has led to a failing educational system, rampant inequality, and incessant fighting among its corrupt and largely inept political leaders. First East Bangladesh broke away in 1971 after a murderous civil war, and now it is deeply divided as various tribes, regions, and different varieties of Islam are engaged in ever more vicious conflicts for control of resources, territory, and the allegiances of their communities. Almost all Pakistanis are Muslims, but aside from the Sunni–Shiite divide, there are various versions of Islam ranging from moderate Sufi Muslims to very extremist jihadists calling for a holy war to create an ultra-religious, intolerant state. Aside from being religiously diverse, Pakistan also has ethnically distinct provinces, some of which are rebellious, while its cities are very mixed and the scene of occasional urban ethnic clashes. The state's failures have opened the way for religious extremists, tribal rebellions, protracted ethnic conflicts, and regional separatism. The only shared basis for nationalist unity that most Pakistanis can agree on is their hostility to and fear of their more powerful and successful neighbor, India. Ultimately, this kind of state failure is extremely dangerous as it can lead a threatened state to try desperately to unite people by concentrating on external enemies. As both Pakistan and India have nuclear weapons, Pakistan's failure to tame its internal divisions could turn into an international tragedy.

The Pakistani case is hardly unique; during much of the 19th and 20th centuries European state leaders used the threat of international danger to nationalize their populations. This was a tactic used by Bismarck to unite Germany and overcome its regional and religious differences, and it led to the creation of a powerful, highly nationalistic, aggressively successful and militarized Germany. That, in turn was one of the reasons for World War I, and Germany's failure in that war in 1918 led to the intense nationalistic resentment. Then there was a devastating inflation in 1923 that ruined much of the German middle class, and after a few years of economic recovery, there was the Great Depression that caused mass unemployment starting in 1930. All this led to Adolf Hitler's rise to power in 1933. He harked back to a mythical past when the German race was pure and great, he blamed Germany's problems on Jews and left-wing traitors, and he promised to make Germany Europe's dominant power. He then launched World War II and the genocide of Jews in 1939.

Memory, Pride, and Solidarity

Economists and most current political scientists who analyze today's ethnic and related kinds of conflicts that lead to civil wars or demands for the establishment of separate states stress economic conditions and rational calculations as keys to understanding why and where these things take place. The presence of a resource base worth capturing is seen as an important cause of regional rebellions or separatism as it causes political leaders to calculate that the risk of war is worth it, given the potential rewards they can capture if they succeed. Also, control of regional resources like diamonds, other minerals, or even products like opium or coffee can finance civil wars. But this highly logical, calculating approach to analyzing communal conflict, while useful, nevertheless misses the importance of less tangible feelings, particularly the resentment felt when a particular group feels it has been demeaned and humiliated; furthermore, the mere memory of such humiliation can be activated generations later and turned into a powerful stimulus to conflict.

The 19th century French historian Ernest Renan wrote that "the essence of a nation is that all individuals have many things in common and also that all have forgotten many things" (Renan's oft-quoted phrase was first said in his lecture on March 11, 1882 at the Sorbonne, "Qu'est-ce qu'une nation"—What is a nation?). By this he meant that the French had to forget the many terrible religious civil wars that had marred their history, the fact that regions with different languages and traditions had been conquered in wars waged by the French state, and that as a result of the French Revolution royalist regions were brutally brought back under control in yet another civil war. There are few modern nations that have not undergone past terrible civil wars that could have led to the formation of different nations. When memories of these events have been overcome, it is not so much that they have been forgotten as that they have been reinterpreted to cool passions and lessen bitter memories.

The United States has done that with its Civil War. For many decades, and to some extent even now, that exceedingly bloody war (called "the war between the states" by White Southerners), actually fought to preserve slavery, was turned into a kind of romantic event with glorious cavalry charges and gallant Southern gentlemen bravely defending states' rights and their way of life. Why this forgetting, or better, reinterpretation works sometimes but not always is not entirely clear. In the United States, as the Civil War was reinterpreted in the late 19th century, part of what was overlooked was that the main issue was slavery, and the South was allowed to impose segregation in order to limit Blacks' freedoms, while the rest of the country accepted the ideology of Black inferiority. Even in the 21st century a good many Southern American Whites continue to believe in the mythology that theirs was a noble cause, and this has contributed to sustaining a special sense of regional distinction that remains an important fact in America's political life, though this does not threaten national unity.

In Belgium, one of Europe's richest countries, from the time of its founding as a state in 1830 until the latter part of the 20th century, French speakers concentrated in the south claimed to be culturally superior to their Flemish (Dutch-speaking) countrymen concentrated in the north. The French part was more economically advanced and had greater cultural prestige. But in recent decades the Flemish part has become richer, and the accumulated bitterness of having been humiliated for over a century has led to the emergence of a strong separatist, Flemish nationalist movement that makes unified governance of Belgium practically impossible. There is no war or violence, partly because of Belgium's continuing prosperity, but for practical purposes there is no such thing as genuine Belgian nationalism and the state is divided by mutual ethnic contempt and memories of past slights.

Nationalist histories regularly exaggerate or simply invent the antiquity of their nation, downplay internal ethnic, religious, and regional differences, and pretend that the emergence of their nation was both inevitable and necessary. Modern scholarship emphasizes that national identities are constructed, and while some existed long ago, all modern ones have been reworked, expanded, or in many cases simply created relatively recently. Also, there is hardly anything "natural" about the overwhelming majority of state or national boundaries as most have been settled by wars and political accidents, not by any neat ethnic or linguistic boundaries. Nationalist myths try to show that past ethnic or other divisions within the nation were temporary, unnatural errors, whereas the reality is that it took great effort and frequent conflicts to create enough cultural homogeneity to sustain nationalist unity. But the reality in no way diminishes the power of historical myths that come to be widely accepted. They become real facts and can play a useful role in taming internal disputes by mitigating ethnic, religious, or regional animosities.

An interesting African case of such a success is mainland Tanzania (leaving aside its autonomous island region of Zanzibar that has had serious ethnic divisions). There, almost uniquely in post-colonial Africa, the European colonial language, English, ceased to be the main national language. It was replaced by Swahili, tribal or ethnic politics were forbidden, and every effort was made to make sure that no single ethnic group (there are over 100) could dominate. Despite a poor record of economic growth, mainland Tanzania has avoided the terrible ethnic conflicts that have beset almost all of its African neighbors. Its first, longtime leader, Julius Nyerere, was also one of Africa's least corrupt and most moderate leaders, and this certainly helped as well. So, the deliberate construction of a story of national solidarity overcoming ethnic divisions is becoming a reality, and national pride is enhanced by the fact that almost uniquely Tanzania's most widely spoken national language is African, not European.

Historical myths, even if they are contrived, and national pride are therefore a double-edged sword. They can contribute to national unity and overcome serious identity conflicts within the state, but they can also lead to prejudice against unassimilated internal minorities and hostility toward the state's external neighbors.

Uniting Against Others: The Mixed Consequences of Nationalism

Despite some exceptions, in most cases national unity has not been achieved by benevolent means. What best unites a nation is external threats, just as what once united tribes, or still brings together ethnic and religious communities is the perception that they are in such danger that they need to present a united front against the enemy. External threats, whether real or invented, overcome internal dissension. Wars and deadly competition between European states greatly contributed to strengthening modern nationalism, just as European colonialism both created and strengthened nationalism in the rest of the world. This is a rather alarming conclusion because it means that overcoming internal conflicts between competing communities can most easily be done by demonizing outsiders.

It is not even necessary for outsiders to be foreigners, as internal minorities can be represented as tools of dangerous other powers. Early English nationalism emerged as anti-Catholicism in the 16th century, though this nationalism was not consolidated until later in wars with other European powers. Romanian nationalism in the 19th century focused on the substantial Jewish minority as an internal enemy, making Romania a willing accomplice in the German-led Holocaust against Jews during World War II. Cambodian nationalism in the 20th century was deeply anti-Vietnamese, and this eventually led to genocidal ethnic cleansing. Modern Turkish nationalism defined those who were not Muslim as non-Turks even though Ataturk, the founder of that nation, insisted on running a secular government. Subsequently, those ethnic and linguistic groups that did not become sufficiently Turkish, notably the Kurds, were told that they did not exist. As most non-Muslims were forced to leave, and most other minorities assimilated into "Turkishness," the Kurdish problem has remained as Turkey's most important ethnic problem and caused episodes of serious internal warfare. We have seen that almost the only thing that can unite Pakistanis is their fear of India, with which they have had three major wars and countless violent skirmishes.

If nationalism defines some communities within the state as outsiders, to be treated intolerantly, conflict will occur and minorities can suffer terrible consequences. Tolerant strategies sometimes work, but some ethnic or religious groups refuse to be assimilated, especially if they feel they have been sinned against. To overcome internal differences, it is useful to concentrate on external enemies, but this can easily increase international tensions.

Nationalism is widespread and necessary to hold states together in the modern world. It is also deeply entangled with issues of ethnicity and sometimes religion. Consequently, any analysis of these phenomena is bound to be full of paradoxes. Nationalism is an important source of unity that can overcome communal conflict or render it harmless, but it also can be a source of increased ethnic and religious discrimination and war. Ethnic awareness may be a positive way of allowing various communities to defend themselves and claim their rights in the modern world, but it can also cause deadly conflicts. Religious feelings, especially in the major religions, can overcome ethnic prejudices by insisting that all believers should be treated well, but it can divide communities and lead to extreme violence. This is why analysts are so divided about how to evaluate nationalism, ethnicity, and religion, with some emphasizing their negative aspects, others the positive, while many are ambivalent.

We will return to how the complex interactions between nations, ethnic groups, and religious communities in our world produce areas of conflict as well as more hopeful situations. First, however, we must digress a bit to explain the most extreme form of ethnic violence that leads to genocide. This is a rare phenomenon, but when it has occurred so many have been slaughtered that it is not something that can be ignored.

DISCUSSION QUESTIONS

1. Why do some political leaders emphasize threats to their communities, and what effect does this have if they convince many that such threats are real? Give an example.
2. What are some of the conditions that aggravate conflicts between ethnicities, religious groups, or different regions within a state? Give an example of a case where this happened.
3. What role does historical memory play in aggravating or mitigating conflicts between different communities? Give an example of each kind of case.

V: Genocides

The Extreme Cases of Ethnic and Religious Conflicts

Looking at genocidal massacres will not only allow us to understand these better, but also point the way to a more hopeful conclusion that spells out the ways in which to diminish conflict.

Though the term genocide first appeared in print only in 1944 to describe what was happening to the Jews in German-occupied Europe during World War II, the phenomenon is much older. Murdering all of a targeted group—men, women, children—because its members share a common ethnicity, religion, nationality, or simply because they all happen to be in the same place has been going on for a long time. The Bible describes genocides of the tribes or ethnic groups called Amalekites, Canaanites, and Midianites (though in this last case virgin women were to be spared to be distributed among Moses' men) in response to the Lord's commandments to wipe them out for religious reasons. Caesar massacred certain tribes in Gaul in the 1st century B.C.E. if they did not surrender and accept Roman rule. In the late 11th century Western Crusaders slaughtered the people in Jerusalem, mostly Muslims and Jews, when they seized it. Other Crusaders from northern France wiped out entire populations of some of the southern French towns they conquered during their war against Albigensian heretics, following orders from the Pope's emissaries. This was to exterminate a Christian heresy, but it was also part of the northern conquest of a part of what would become France that spoke a different language than in the north. Mongols in the 13th century sometimes ordered massacres of entire cities if these had not surrendered or were believed to have betrayed prior agreements, and Tamerlane, a Turkic Muslim ruler descendant from the Mongols, did the same in Central Asia and Persia a century later. European conquerors killed whole tribes in the Americas and Australia; and though it was not genocide in the sense that the intent was not to kill them all, millions of Africans captured as slaves to be brought to the Americas died in the process of being transported and from being overworked.

In the 20th century, we have already listed the major genocides in Table 3.1 (category F), though some episodes were left out because they were prompted by factors other than the ones being studied in this book. Stalin, the Communist dictator of the Soviet Union, ordered the massacre of better-off peasant families in the Soviet Union in the late 1920s and 1930s by direct killing, forced starvation, and deportation in conditions that killed most of those targeted, but the basis for targeting them was their economic position, not ethnicity or religion. Later, Stalin deported many minority ethnic and national groups to Siberia because he did not trust them, and vast numbers, millions more, died in the process, though the intent was not to kill all of them. Mao Zedong, China's Communist dictator, did the same thing in the 1950s to more prosperous peasants and landlords, and also caused up to 30 million more deaths in the Great Leap Forward because of grotesquely bad economic policies forced on his country. But again, this kind of mass politically motivated murder is not the kind we are analyzing. That still leaves the other cases that were based on conflicts between or prejudices against ethnic or religious communities identified as "others" who did not belong in the nation.

Only the naive can suppose that such episodes, because they are fairly rare, can somehow be explained as peculiar psychological abnormalities or sickness. The fact is that certain kinds of conditions combined with intolerant ideological mindsets always have the potential to produce such ghastly outcomes. What are these?

First, there are genocides of pure convenience and greed. Aboriginal tribes in Australia had their lands taken away and they fought back, though they were too few and too poorly armed to do much against British settlers. So, wiping them out was an easy and convenient way of getting those out of the way who would not settle into confining reservations. Enlightenment ideals expounded by Europeans and enshrined in the notion that all of us have the right to life and liberty would not consider this legitimate, but European colonizers often considered less technologically advanced people as racial inferiors, and in some cases as barely human at all. There were always some Europeans who protested, but at least until the late 19th century, such tragedies were deemed acceptable, though today they are not.

A second cause of genocidal mass murder of targeted groups is revenge. They did something to us, supposedly, so we have the right to do it to them. This has happened often in warfare, though usually at a local level. One of the most egregious 20th century cases was the Japanese systematic slaughter of hundreds of thousands of Chinese in the city of Nanjing after they seized it in December 1937. Mass rape, torture, and executions took place, not because Japanese soldiers were out of control, but under orders by the high command that was avenging prior Chinese resistance even though Nanjing itself had not resisted. Some ask if the firebombing of German and Japanese cities toward the end of World War II and the use of atomic bombs on Japan were primarily caused by a desire for revenge. But neither Germany nor Japan had surrendered when these events took place, whereas in Nanjing the city had surrendered and almost all those killed were civilians. Unlike with the Allied bombings of Germany and Japan, the death toll in Nanjing could hardly be claimed as unfortunate "collateral damage." Japan's ideology at the time was very explicitly and virulently racist, claiming that the Japanese race was inherently superior and had every right to brutally conquer the rest of Asia.

A third and very potent cause of genocides is the sense that if "we" don't do it to "them," they will do it to us. This was the thinking of the Ottoman authorities who ordered the ethnic cleansing and mass killing of Armenians in Anatolia in 1915. The Ottoman Empire was losing in World War I and its leaders feared that an Armenian independence movement allied to the advancing Russian army would create an independent Armenia. This would destroy the Empire and subject its Muslim population to expulsion and killing. That the great majority of Christian Armenians killed were ordinary people unconnected to such political schemes made no difference. In fact, the rise of modern nationalism contributed greatly because the establishment of independent nations supposed some sort of ethnic homogeneity, and nations were increasingly fearful of potentially disloyal ethnicities. By 1915 the leaders of the Ottoman Empire saw themselves as Muslim Turkish nationalists who could not trust the Christian ethnic groups they had ruled relatively peacefully for many centuries before nationalism had infected them.

When Hutus turned on Tutsis and tried to massacre all of them in 1994, the reason was similar. The ruling Hutu elite feared that as long as any Tutsi remained, they would claim a share or perhaps all power. There was a rebel Tutsi army advancing on them, and they feared dire consequences if they lost the war. So they decided that eliminating the Tutsi population would make it impossible for the rebels to take power.

The fourth and most sinister reason is the fear of pollution. This was clearly the reason given in the Bible for wiping out the Canaanites. The fear was that if they remained, Jewish men might mingle with their women, and soon accept their gods, thus denying the monopoly of belief demanded by the one true God. The slaughter of Albigensian heretics in the 13th century was similar. So were the extreme cruelty and frequent massacres during the Protestant–Catholic wars of religion that raged in parts of Europe, including France and Ireland in the 16th and 17th century. There were more prosaic reasons for much of the killing—greed and competition for power—but the ferocity and scope of some of the massacres in which everyone in certain captured towns was slaughtered went beyond this. A sense that God wanted the earth cleansed of heresy was what made these religious wars so vicious. Cromwell's English Protestant troops actually held up the Book of Joshua, in which the slaughter of Canaanites is demanded, as their model as they massacred Irish Catholics.

The most terrible such episode in modern times was the Holocaust. Anti-Semitism is an ancient prejudice, and it was strengthened in late 19th century Europe by the perception that emancipated Jews were disproportionately benefiting by the advance of capitalism and the success of the industrial revolution. As this upset many traditions, favored urban over rural values and populations, and threatened the hold of traditional religion, Jews were increasingly blamed for the unsettling rapidity of social change. To this were added new biological interpretations that twisted Darwin's theory of evolution and Pasteur's discovery of invisible germs as the cause of disease. Jews, some began to say, were like an insidious disease poisoning society and pure European races, thus fatally weakening their capacity to survive. All sorts of pseudo-scientific arguments were advanced to claim that only pure races could survive (though this had nothing to do with Darwinian theories), that Jews were engaged in mysterious plots to take over the world, and that mixing with others was part of their plan. This was a time, in the late 19th and early 20th century when racial theories were widely believed, and Europeans considered themselves to be biologically superior. Hitler and his Nazis took this a step further, claiming that to insure racial purity for Aryan Germans every Jew had to be destroyed, otherwise they could insidiously reproduce, like a virus, and pollute the world once more.

The destruction of one quarter of Cambodia's population by the Communists, called the Khmer Rouge, during their rule from 1975 to 1979, followed a somewhat similar logic, though it also mixed in all the other murderous ideological currents of the 20th century. First, the Khmer Rouge believed the historical myth that their ancestors had produced a great Khmer civilization by being united into a vast rice-growing nation, but then had been undermined by foreign intrusions from Thailand and Vietnam. They believed that they could reunite their nation by purifying it of foreign elements, and make it into a superior race once more. They also accepted a central point of communist ideology, that certain classes were more fit than others, and that those who were in the way had to be eliminated. They turned this into a kind of ethnic concept through which whole families of the condemned classes, namely those polluted by foreign and urban influences, had to be wiped out. So, they went after Cambodia's minorities, first of all the Vietnamese, then the Cham. They destroyed the cities and people who had lived in them. They went after all those who had been polluted by exposure to Vietnamese influence of any sort, real or imagined. They herded the remaining population into inefficient rural communes to work as forced laborers as they imagined their Khmer ancestors had worked. Finally, they turned against their most powerful neighbor, Vietnam, even though it was also ruled by Communists. Their ultra-nationalist claim was that centuries earlier southern Vietnam had been part of the Khmer Empire, so it should be once more. This was one step too far, and the far larger, better-armed Vietnam countered by invading Cambodia and overthrowing the Khmer Rouge in 1979. But by then, close to two million people had been butchered and starved to death.

So this was partly the result of a modern nationalism that relied on a mythological, heroic version of Cambodian history, on racist theories about the dangers of pollution and mixing, on extreme xenophobic hatred of everything foreign, and on an ideology that claimed that as a superior race they could do anything, even vanquish bigger and stronger neighbors. The Khmer Rouge also benefited from a widespread Cambodian sense of resentment at having been pushed around by stronger neighbors, then colonized by the French, and in the early 1970s, bombed by the Americans as part of the Vietnam War. Aside from the fact that the Khmer Rouge added communist theories of economic class to the mix, the rest was quite similar to the German Nazis who also used mixtures of mythical history, deep resentment over Germany's failures, racial theories, and a sense of their own absolute superiority to try to conquer the world. Some of the same elements of a fabricated history, resentment about past wrongs, and racist theories were present as well in Rwanda.

Genocides have been rare, but studying them highlights the conditions that lead to lesser conflicts and shows that a sense of racial, ethnic, or religious superiority can lead to intolerant attitudes without necessarily producing genocides. So can resentment of other groups, or fear. Then prejudices and distrust harden long before actual genocides take place. Finally, even a sense that another group is somehow polluting need not be so extreme as to lead to massacres, but it can contribute to attitudes that make ethnic conflict more likely. Fear of racial mixing was prevalent among White American Southerners for a long time as well as among South African Whites. So we can take these attitudes, look at where they exist, and get some sense of potentially serious ethnic, religious, and national conflicts today. We can also better understand how combating certain beliefs can make it easier to mitigate conflict or make it less likely.

DISCUSSION QUESTIONS

1. What are the four main causes of genocide?
2. Name and briefly explain the origins of three genocides over the past 100 years.
3. How does the study of genocides actually help us understand less violent conflicts, and also point the way to making such conflicts less dangerous?

VI: Contemporary Dangers and Opportunities

⤙⤙✕⤚⤚

T he great change that occurred as agrarian empires and kingdoms were transformed into modern states put a premium on much greater loyalty and identification with the state. It is not that agrarian states were always so tolerant because, as we have seen, there were deadly episodes of religious fanaticism that resulted in bitter wars and massacres. But generally, these states did not expect much from their subjects, only taxes and political passivity. Modern states, however, want much more from their subjects in order to make war, modernize their economies, and provide political support, while subject populations also demand more services, opportunities, and direct help from their states. Modernizing economies need to enlist better-educated and culturally more homogeneous labor forces. Education systems have to be set up, all sorts of new bureaucracies have to be staffed and paid for, and order has to be maintained in the rapidly growing cities that can no longer rely on the kind of traditional village solidarity that used to keep people relatively safe. This is why nationalizing projects have been a central aspect of political life in the new states that emerged from fallen agrarian empires in the 19th and 20th centuries, because without them states cannot count on the support they need from those they rule.

Nationalism, however, ran into the problem of ethnically and religiously mixed populations that were characteristic of almost all larger agrarian states, especially in urban centers. Furthermore, the early stages of **modernization** saw large-scale migration into growing cities so that many of them became more mixed than ever. This made the treatment of minorities a crucial issue as various ethnically and religiously defined communities competed for resources. As some groups who were culturally better adapted to urban, modern life did better than others, resentment of their success made the situation even more difficult, especially if those who did well were minorities within the emerging nations. Chinese migrants into Southeast Asia, Jews in Europe, Ibos in Nigeria, Armenians and Greeks in the late Ottoman Empire, Indians in eastern Africa, and many other cases are good examples. At the same time, ethnicities that spoke the favored national languages received more opportunities in education and for government jobs, thus creating resentment among those left out. The rise of modern nationalism consequently created grounds for new ethnic conflicts.

The Unmixing and Remixing of Populations

Intolerant nationalist projects handled the problems of ethnic and religious mixing poorly, and we have seen that this led in many European cases and in Turkey to a great "unmixing" of populations. Those not deemed to be part of the nation were subject to persecution, expulsions, and genocidal massacres. World War II, the Holocaust, forced migrations after the War, and changes in boundaries made eastern and central European nation-states more homogeneous. The last, dramatic episode like this in Europe was the multi-sided Yugoslav civil war of the 1990s.

It was not just in Europe that great unmixings took place. India fell into large-scale war, forced migration, and killing at the time of its independence, and part of the horrible Khmer Rouge period in Cambodia was aimed very specifically at ridding the country of non-Khmers and foreign influence. Continuing ethnic conflicts in many parts of Africa and the Middle East are caused by exactly the same drive to forge nations out of disparate populations.

But unmixing can only go so far. For one thing, improved transportation, rapid economic advances, and the large gap in wealth between rich and poor countries and regions have vastly increased migration. More economically advanced nations that slowly and painfully achieved a greater level of cultural homogeneity have now begun to find themselves increasingly diverse. This is most evident in the rich West European nation-states such as France where over 7 percent of the population is now Muslim. In 1950, almost all of the French were Catholics who spoke fluent French. There was a small Protestant minority, a smaller Jewish one, and a few regions where local languages were still spoken, but little of this seemed problematic, and there was general agreement that practically everyone was loyal to the French nation. This is no longer true, and the same holds for most West European nations today.

Migration is a fact of life throughout the world. Burmese refugees are pouring into richer Thailand; the oil-rich Arabian states have very large foreign populations who do much of the crucial work; Central Americans migrate to richer Mexico, and Mexicans as well as Central Americans move to the United States. Poor Chinese come to North America, Europe, and Japan; Eastern Europeans are moving to Western Europe; Somalis are fleeing their devastated land and appearing in neighboring African countries, in Europe, and in the United States, and so on. Growing ethnic misunderstanding and nationalist reactions against immigrants are now a fact of life in many parts of the world. The trend toward unmixing has been reversed, raising the question of how established nation-states will handle culturally different immigrants and their descendants.

The Return of Religious Conflict

World War I was a war between competing nation-states. World War II was that and also a matter of mutually incompatible ideologies. The Cold War and the peripheral wars it spawned in Korea, Vietnam, Afghanistan, Angola, and others was ideological, though at the local level in Afghanistan and Angola Cold War conflicts were also between various ethnic groups. Still, the main contending world ideologies, democracy, capitalism, communism, and fascism were secular, not religious. Religion certainly played a role in the India–Pakistani wars and continuing hostility, but ethnicity and nationalism were at stake as well. The same was true in the Yugoslav, Sri Lankan, and Sudanese civil wars where ethnic and separatist nationalist claims seemed far more important than the fact that different sides in these conflicts also had different religious traditions. Most of the many civil wars in the second half the 20th century that occurred in Latin America, Africa, and Asia were fought over matters of secular ideology and the distribution of economic benefits, and often, but not always, between ethnic communities struggling to gain control of states or regions and their resources. So it seemed that religious identities were becoming increasingly irrelevant.

Now, in the early 21st century, it is becoming clear that it is not so. Religious differences are coming to the fore once more as a principal cause of conflict. Though the news is not welcome, it is difficult to deny that there is a growing sense of frustration and anger among Muslims in many parts of the world, and that extremist versions of Islam are gaining ground. They are demanding that Muslims abandon their loyalty to secular nationalism and replace it with their religious identities. This poses a very severe challenge to Muslim societies, but it also has become a highly globalized issue because of the spread of Muslim communities into many parts of the world where before they were not present. Are Muslim minorities going to be primarily loyal to the states in which they reside? Will they be sufficiently assimilated?

A large part of the problem is that few Muslim states have managed to satisfy the material and social aspirations of their people. We have sketched out the situation in Pakistan, and with some variation, it could be repeated throughout most of the Middle East, particularly in Arab countries. In the aftermath of decolonization and newly gained independence, discontent was captured by secular, nationalist, and socialist movements promising rapid modernization and appealing to national pride. Nasser in Egypt and the Ba'athist movement in Syria and Iraq epitomized this. But these secular movements, and similar ones in Algeria and Libya, failed to deliver the goods. Perhaps just as importantly, they were unable to produce promised national greatness. The Arab failure to defeat Israel exposed humiliating weakness. This left an ideological gap that was filled by ultra-religious movements whose promise was that if Muslims would go back to their pure original faith God would once again make Islam as strong as it had been centuries earlier. This would wipe away the shame of having been colonized by the Christian West, and the continuing failure to eliminate what many consider to be the West's last alien colony in the Muslim world, Israel.

In 1979 an Islamic revolution brought religious extremists to power in Iran, but Iran is Shiite, something most Muslims, who are overwhelmingly Sunni, consider to be a heresy. This opened up the long-standing wound in much of the Middle East and

Pakistan where Sunnis had long treated Shiites as inferiors. Over the past few decades violent conflicts between these two religious identities has broken out in many places, most of all in Iraq, but also in Lebanon, Pakistan, and Yemen.

Even where there is no such conflict, as in Algeria or Egypt, religious extremists have turned to violence in order to overthrow governments they consider corrupt and insufficiently pious. At least 100,000 have died in Algeria in what amounts to a civil war between Islamists and a more secularly minded political elite.

For Muslim immigrants in Western Europe, the revival of religious fervor and tensions in their home countries, and the fact that they suffer from prejudice have combined to encourage a small but growing number of their young to turn to religious extremism. Most of the terrorism directed against Western countries has been carried out by precisely these young immigrants seething with resentment against the Christian West, against Jews, and against the countries where they have settled because they believe they have been unfairly treated.

But it is not just within Islam that religious extremism has grown. Christian fundamentalism has flourished in the United States, in Africa, and in many parts of Latin America. In the case of Africa violence between evangelical Christians and increasingly radicalized Muslims has increased. In India a kind of Hindu religious extremism has also developed. It is largely directed against the very large Muslim minority within India.

When religious differences coincide with ethnic ones, as is the case with Muslim immigrants in the West who are identified as Turks, Pakistanis, Arabs, Kurds, or others, then conflict takes on a particularly sharp aspect.

Given all this, what strategies are available to mitigate these new ethnic, religious, and nationalist tensions? We can go back to Table 2.1 and ask how to promote tolerant solutions because clearly those are the ones with a better chance of avoiding or mitigating conflict and preventing or at least reducing violence.

Promoting Tolerant Solutions

We need to acknowledge that in today's world nationalism is the only emotional force that binds together disparate communities and identities in order to reduce conflict within states. At the same time, the excesses of nationalism have to be recognized. Internally nationalist pride and prejudice can engender persecution of minorities and lead to conflict. Nationalism can lead to jingoism, excessive pride in one's own nation and contempt for others. This has in the past produced excessive militarization of the states and war.

Tolerant assimilation, on the other hand, often works if given time. There is ample evidence, for example, that in Western Europe a growing number of second- and now third-generation descendants of Muslim immigrants have assimilated. They speak the national languages, increasingly participate in democratic politics, and see their religious identities as secondary to their national ones. Any kind of attempt to force the issue by insisting on hasty assimilation is more likely to backfire. Even worse are moves that justify prejudice against Muslims, or even exclude them from mainstream society.

The United States has hardly had a blameless record in its dealings with ethnic minorities, whether voluntary immigrants, Native Americans, or African-Americans. But it has had enough of a tradition of tolerant assimilation to serve as a useful model for how this can be done. Since the 1960s, the United States has also practiced affirmative action, which promotes members of minorities to higher positions in order to achieve a better balance at the elite level. Much criticized by many, either because it has not done enough to redress past injustices, or from the other side because it seems unfair to consider ethnicity, race, or gender in deciding on promotions, the strategy has worked. Its main advantage is that it has allowed the most able members of minorities, particularly African-Americans, to advance, and thus made it far less likely that they would turn their attention to enlisting their ethnic group in a violent struggle against the state. Affirmative action, in other words, gives hope to poorly assimilated minorities and creates leaders who are more loyal to the larger nation than to separatist or violently oppositional movements. (Americans often call this multiculturalism, but it is not. Rather, it is a form of tolerant assimilation.)

There are cases, however, where even the most tolerant assimilation policy is not enough, particularly if a minority ethnic group is in the majority in a particular region of the state, or if it refuses to be assimilated. Then tolerant multiculturalism, as practiced in most (but not all) parts of India, in Canada, or as is being tried in South Africa (with as yet mixed results) offers far more hope than pushing for either forced assimilation or simply trying to hold down the disaffected region or minority by force.

In the end, when all else fails, peaceful separation of regions, where feasible, and the establishment of new nation-states, as happened in Czechoslovakia, is a better solution than endless war and repression, as in Sudan. This requires a willingness by the dominant nation to give up territory, unlike what happened in Yugoslavia where Serbia tried to hold on to insurgent areas by force.

In other words, each situation has to be looked at separately. All compromises have costs and create moral dilemmas. Giving up too much territory can drastically weaken a state so that previously stable nations break up into newly awakened ethnic regions. Multiculturalism works as long as it does not undermine national solidarity by encouraging previously minor and weak differences to be accentuated and lead to fragmentation as all sorts of groups begin to make their own separate demands.

Aside from saying that toleration works better in most cases than intolerant solutions, we must recognize that effective states and successful economies are an important part of any solution. Highly corrupt states, policies that impede economic progress, and governments too weak to prevent outside intervention that arms particular ethnic, religious, or regional groups against the state make any kind of solution to internal conflicts very difficult. How to make governance cleaner and more effective, and what kinds of economic policies work best are fascinating questions that go far beyond the scope of our concerns here, but it is useful to remember that they are relevant.

That leaves the question of how to promote tolerance of differences so that compromises and workable, less confrontational solutions can be found to the problems of ethnic, religious, and national conflicts.

Ethnic, religious, and national identities are variable. We have seen that nationalism can exist now where it did not in the past. This is true for religious and ethnic identities as well. The United States has created, for example, an ethnicity called "Asian-American" that includes people originally from India, Vietnam, China, and many other Asian places. Of course, in Asia itself this term has little meaning as the many different nationalities and ethnic groups on that continent have their own distinct identities. Two hundred years ago, there was no "Italy" or "Germany," only sets of different states and regions with their own distinct cultures, histories, and languages. Some of the ethnic groups called tribes in Africa did not share a common identity in the past, but because of cultural and linguistic similarities came to recognize themselves as such when some of them moved to the new colonial cities and looked for support among those most like themselves. So we know that strong new identities can be created, and old ones gradually eliminated.

Recognizing that even groups with strong identities have in the past resulted from mixtures and blending of various people makes it less likely they will insist on keeping themselves separate or believe that they need to exclude those who don't quite fit in. Any kind of exclusive claim to having been "pure" for very long periods of time in the past raises the risk of intolerance and a closed attitude toward compromising with others. Making historical claims based on myths that pretend that "we" have been here forever, or are a biologically fixed group with closed boundaries makes it more likely that any kind of conflict will be harder to resolve.

It is not so much that it is necessary to forget history as it is to accept the contingent nature of group solidarity and to think less about the need to set fixed boundaries against others. Honest history rather than ethnic, religious, or nationalist stories that emphasize resentment over past real or imagined affronts lessens the likelihood that conflicts will become more violent. On the other hand, cultivating a desire for revenge and basing a particular identity's solidarity on a shared sense of persecution stokes that group's anger and fear. We know that ethnic, or for that matter religious and nationalist political entrepreneurs looking for support try to mobilize their followers by claiming that their community is being persecuted and threatened. The more such appeals succeed, the less likely it is that disputes with other ethnic groups, religions, or nations will be resolved peacefully. So, making people aware of the dangers of exaggerating threats can make an important contribution to easing tensions and reducing the appeal of those political leaders whose popularity depends on promoting fear and resentment.

A central point of Enlightenment thinking in the 18th century was the belief that dogma—unthinking acceptance of any ideology—blinds people to rational solutions. All of modern science is based on the notion that there is no final and unalterable truth based on some text or pronouncement by the authorities. Rather, received knowledge has to be tested, and may, in the long run, turn out to be different from what was once supposed.

Absolute certitude that one's ideology is perfectly true, and all others are inherently worthless is a sure way to make compromise and understanding of others' positions impossible. In that sense, the Enlightenment's demand for some modesty to replace dogmatic belief is a valuable attitude for mitigating conflicts between groups.

Recognizing that all of us, whatever group identity we may have, are much alike and fully human is essential for reducing intolerance. Assuming that some others are less human, or irremediably untrustworthy, or dangerous simply by virtue of being part of another ethnicity, religion, or nationality is a prescription for adopting intolerant strategies in dealing with minorities or potentially rival communities. Similarly, accepting the fact that individuals vary, and that the sins of one or several members of a particular group does not mean that all of them are alike makes tolerance more acceptable and probable.

All this can be summarized as a set of propositions:

1. Good governance and rising prosperity make conflict between different identities less likely.
2. Understanding that ethnic, religious, and national identities, however strongly they may be felt, are actually variable and that most present ones resulted from some mixing of people in the past makes it easier to work out tolerant solutions to conflicts between such groups today.
3. Cultivating a sense of persecution and resentment of past wrongs, whether these have been real or are just historical fabrications, is a sure way to make communities more resistant to compromises and toleration of those whose ancestors supposedly committed these wrongs.
4. Political leaders who try to mobilize their communities by instilling fear and stoking resentment are dangerous instigators of intolerance and conflict.
5. Absolute, dogmatic belief that some received ideology about another ethnicity, religion, or nationality is immutably true and can never be doubted makes tolerance and compromise much more difficult.
6. Understanding that we are all human individuals with rights and obligations makes tolerance possible. On the other hand, treating all members of an ethnic, religious, or national community as merely group members without individual personalities makes intolerance far more probable because it assigns to all the members of that group any existing negative associations or resentment for past wrongs. Taken to extremes, denial of individualism, that is lumping all members

of a group into one single group identity makes genocidal mass killing possible in cases of very severe group conflict.

Writing this and calling for education to teach these principles is easy. Convincing those whose thinking leads them to intolerance, resentment, and fear is extremely difficult. Reforming institutions that block good governance and progress, or that promote intolerance and conflict is not only difficult, but very time consuming. Understanding all this is only a first step, but a necessary one.

DISCUSSION QUESTIONS

1. What is meant by the "unmixing" and "remixing" of populations in the modern world?
2. Where in today's world is religion becoming an increasing cause of political conflict?
3. What are some educational policies that could promote more tolerant solutions to ethnic and religious conflicts, and what important role can teaching history play in either aggravating or easing such conflicts?

Bibliography

Though there is considerable overlap in the scholarship on nationalism, ethnic conflict, and religious conflict, this bibliography places books in the category each work most emphasizes. The list below includes only a very small sample of the thousands of works on these subjects, but it does list some of the most important books published in the past three decades.

On Nationalism

Anderson, Benedict. 2006. *Imagined Communities*, 3rd edition. London: Verso.

Breuilly, John. 1993. *Nationalism and the State*, 2nd edition. Chicago: University of Chicago Press.

Brubaker, Rogers. 1996. *Nationalism Reframed*. Cambridge: Cambridge University Press

Connor, Walker. 1994. *Ethnonationalism*. Princeton: Princeton University Press.

Geary, Patrick. 2002. *The Myth of Nations*. Princeton: Princeton University Press.

Gellner, Ernest. 2006. *Nations and Nationalism*, 2nd edition. Oxford: Blackwell.

Greenfeld, Liah. 1992. *Nationalism*. Cambridge: Harvard University Press.

Hobsbawm, Eric. 1992. *Nations and Nationalism since 1780*. Cambridge: Cambridge University Press.

Kedourie, Elie. 1993. *Nationalism*, 4th edition. Oxford: Blackwell.

Smith, Anthony. 1986. *The Ethnic Origins of Nations*. Oxford: Blackwell.

On Ethnicity and Ethnic Conflict

Chirot, Daniel, and Clark McCauley. 2010. *Why Not Kill Them All?* 2nd edition. Princeton: Princeton University Press.

Collier, Paul. 2009. *Wars, Guns, and Votes*. New York: Harper Collins.

Esman, Milton. 2004. *An Introduction to Ethnic Conflict*. Cambridge: Polity Press.

Hale, Henry. 2008. *The Foundations of Ethnic Politics*. Cambridge: Cambridge University Press.

Horowitz, Donald. 2001. *The Deadly Ethnic Riot*. Berkeley: University of California Press.

Kiernan, Ben. 2007. *Blood and Soil*. New Haven: Yale University Press.

Laitin, David. 2007. *Nations, States, and Violence.* Oxford: Oxford University Press.

Marx, Anthony. 1998. *Making Race and Nation.* Cambridge: Cambridge University Press.

Patterson, Orlando. 1998. *The Ordeal of Integration.* Washington: Civita/Counterpoint.

Prunier, Gerard. 2009. *Africa's World War.* Oxford: Oxford University Press.

Tambiah, Stanley. 1996. *Leveling Crowds.* Berkeley: University of California Press.

Toft, Monica. 2003. *The Geography of Ethnic Violence.* Princeton: Princeton University Press.

Varshney, Ashutosh. 2002. *Ethnic Conflict and Civic Life.* New Haven: Yale University Press.

On Religion and Religious Conflict

Almond, Gabriel, Scott Appleby, and Emanuel Sivan. 2003. *Strong Religion.* Chicago: University of Chicago Press.

Brass, Paul. 1997. *Theft of an Idol.* Princeton: Princeton University Press.

Bruce, Steve. 2000. *Fundamentalism.* Cambridge: Polity Press.

Hefner, Robert, ed. 2005. *Remaking Muslim Politics.* Princeton: Princeton University Press.

Froese, Paul. 2008. *The Plot to Kill God.* Berkeley: University of California Press.

Juergensmeyer, Mark. 2008. *Global Rebellion.* Berkeley: University of California Press.

Nasr, Vali. 2006. *The Shia Revival.* New York: W.W. Norton.

Norris, Pippa, and Ronald Inglehart. 2004. *Sacred and Secular.* Cambridge: Cambridge University Press.

Roy, Olivier. 2010. *Holy Ignorance,* 1st American edition. New York: Columbia University Press.

Stark, Rodney. 1996. *The Rise of Christianity.* Princeton: Princeton University Press.

Glossary/Index

Note: Page numbers followed by "t" refer to tables.

A

affirmative action 49

Afghanistan 8, 47

Africa

  clans in 8–10, 14, 33

  colonialism in 8, 14, 17–18

  discrimination and causes of conflict in 33

  economic failure 33

  increasing religious conflict in 48

  independence in 8, 18

agrarian state: states in the past in which the large majority of people were peasants ruled by small groups of nobles, princes, kings, or emperors. Most people lived in rural villages and were not expected to take part in their state's political system except to pay various kinds of taxes and labor obligations. In return they received some limited security, but little else. 1–3, 45

  see also **empire**, **state**

Algeria 18, 48

American Revolution 13

Ancient Egypt 2, 4, 6

Ancient Greece 6, 16

Angola 18, 47

anti-Semitism: hatred of Jews. In the past this was largely based on religious prejudices, but since the mid-19th century much anti-Semitism has come to be based on pseudo-scientific racial theories claiming that all Jews are inherently undesirable. The attempt by Hitler's Germany and its allies to exterminate all Jews was based on such notions and went so far as to claim that Jews were like a disease poisoning the healthy German race. 16, 42–43

  see also **genocide**, **Nazism**, **race**, **religion**

Armenia 16, 42

assimilation: changing different culturally, ethnically, or religiously defined identities to conform more closely to majority attitudes and values. This is a key part of turning diverse communities into a more homogeneous nation, but it may arouse resistance and lead to conflict. x, 19, 19t, 21, 48–49

see also **integration**

Australia 21, 41

Austro-Hungarian Empire 3, 22, 23

B

Bangladesh 24, 35

Belgium 22, 26t, 37

Belize 26t

Bible 40, 42

Bismarck, Otto von 35

Burkina Faso 26t

Burma 7, 17, 27t

C

Cambodia
> genocide in 28t, 43
> nationalism in 38, 43–44
> unmixing of population 46

Canada 18–19, 26t, 33

Catholic–Protestant conflict
> in 16th and 17th century Europe 7, 38, 42
> in Northern Ireland ix–x, 9, 27t, 28t

Chechnya 27t

China
> conflict in Han areas 26t
> conflict in non-Han areas 27t
> empire 2
> Great Leap Forward 41
> minorities in 19
> Nanjing massacre 41
> religion in 4
> and Tibet 27t, 29t

Christian fundamentalism 48

Christianity
> in European colonial empires 5
> in Roman Empire 4

clan: a group of closely related families claiming to have common ancestors who share a common political solidarity. Larger clans, or groups of clans, can form a whole tribe, but in pre-state societies or weak states, clans were and in some cases remain important political actors. 1, 2

    in Africa 8–10, 14, 33

    see also **tribe**

Cold War 46–47

colonial empires 3

    collapse of 15, 17–18

    European 3, 14, 15

    genocide in 41

    legacy in Africa 8, 17

    rising nationalism in 15, 17

communism: communist ideology was based on the writing of Karl Marx and his followers. It claimed that complete state control of the economy and the elimination of private property would create a happier, more harmonious, egalitarian, and less alienated modern society. In practice Communist regimes were harsh dictatorships. Since 1989, when communism collapsed in Eastern Europe and the Soviet Union, its appeal has decreased. 17

conflict

    and control of resources 36

    discrimination a cause of 32–33

    economic situation and bearing on 33–35

    nationalism and uniting against others 38–39

    and partitioning to prevent 29t

    peaceful resolution of 28–29t

    range of ethnic, religious, or regional 25, 26–28t

    real or imagined threats and 31–32, 35, 38, 50

    return of religious 46–48

    state failures as a major cause of 35–36, 47

    strategies for dealing with 33–35, 48–52

    suppression of 29t

Crusades 40

culture: a set of values, habits, means of expression, and rules of behavior shared by a group of people who recognize that they have these in common, and therefore identify themselves as a community. A common language or religion may be part of a common culture, and they often are. But sometimes several languages or religions may exist harmoniously together within a single cultural identity. x, 1, 2, 5, 7, 12

Cyprus 23–24, 29t

Czechoslovakia 23, 29t

D

de Klerk, F. W. 33

Democratic Republic of Congo 8, 18

discrimination 32–33

E

East Timor 26t, 27t, 28t, 29t

economic prosperity and bearing on conflict 33–35

Egypt

    Ancient 2, 4, 6

    conflict with violence but no war 27t

    religious extremists in 48

elite: economic elites, or upper classes, are wealthy and control much of their society's economy. Political elites have power and are able to enforce that through the use of force; they also try to gain economic and cultural elite status. Religious elites are thought to possess greater access to the divine. There are elites whose position rests on their cultural prestige that can be inherited, or gained by their accomplishments. 2

    affirmative action to achieve racial balance of 49

    languages of 12

    loyalty to state 6, 8

    powers questioned by Enlightenment philosophy 13

    ruling of agrarian states 3

emigrant

    see **immigrant/emigrant**

empire: a state that rules many different kinds of people, most of whom have some local autonomy within their communities but do not have much say in the overall politics of that state. Imperial elites therefore rule disparate kinds of ethnicities, tribes, cultures, and potential nations without giving them the right to have their own sovereign states. Agrarian empires ruled much of the pre-modern world, and Europeans created colonial empires that ruled most of the world until roughly the middle of the 20th century. 2–3

    see also colonial empires

English nationalism, early 38

Enlightenment: from the late 1600s to the early 1800s European philosophers developed new theories about how to organize social life. Recognition of individual rights, promoting freedom of thought, and a belief in the utility of evidence-based science were its key principles. 13, 15, 41, 51

Eritrea 23, 29t

Estonia 26t

Ethiopia 23, 29t

ethnic cleansing: forced expulsion of an ethnically defined community in order to leave an area populated only by groups deemed desirable by those in power. There have been many examples of religiously defined groups expelled in similar ways. Typically, ethnic cleansing is done by force and results in large numbers of fatalities, so that it often verges on or becomes actual genocide. 16, 17, 23, 42

see also **genocide**

ethnic entrepreneurs 31

ethnic group: people who believe they share a common biological ancestry, even though quite often this belief is based on myths or legends that were invented to create a sense of solidarity. Those with a common ethnic identity usually share a common culture as well. ix–x, 1

see also **nation**, **race**, **tribe**

F

failed state: there are geographic areas today where state institutions have collapsed and political competition for resources takes place between contending ethnic groups, tribes, or clans. In a number of states there exist formal governments, but they are incapable of delivering either basic security or the services modern governments are expected to provide, so these can also be called failed or partially failed states. x, 8–10

see also **nation-state**, **state**

fascism: an authoritarian, ultra-nationalist, and militarist ideology that emerged in the 20th century. Fascist governments led their counties into wars of conquest justified by the assertion that their nations were somehow superior and entitled to rule others. Fascism appealed widely in parts of Latin America and Asia before World War II, but the defeat of the major Fascist powers in World War II decreased its appeal. 17

see also **Nazism**

Finland 26t

France

    collapse of empire 17

    Crusaders in 40

    French Revolution 12, 13, 36

    immigrant population 46

    Wars of Religion 42

G

genocide: the targeted killing of any community defined by its culture, ethnicity, religion, nationality, or sometimes economic class. This means that all of those in that group of people—men, women, children—are slated for extermination, not just combatants. The word genocide was invented to describe the attempt by Germany to exterminate the Jews during World War II, but the practice is ancient, and has continued into our own times. 16, 21, 40–44

H

I

immigrant/emigrant: immigrants are people who enter a territory from another one. Today that usually means moving from one sovereign state into another, but it can also mean moving from one region to another. Emigrants are those who leave their homes for another territory. x, 5, 10

Kashmir problem 10, 27t, 32

minorities in 7, 19

multiculturalism in 21

relations with Pakistan 35, 38

religion in 4, 5

religious extremists in 31–32, 48

Indochina 17

Indonesia

conflict in 26t, 27t, 28t, 29t

independence in 17–18

industrialization: the shift from primarily rural, agrarian kinds of economies to ones based first on the use of mechanical power to vastly increase production of goods, and more recently, the eventual shift to economies that also provide far greater numbers of services to raise standards of living. Industrialization began in northwestern Europe, starting in England, but subsequently spread throughout the rest of the world. 11, 12

see also **modernization**

integration/segregation: modern nation-states seek to integrate various ethnic, religious, and regional identities into a single national one. In some cases, however, some groups defined as being different because of their ethnicity or religion are kept partly separate in an inferior status. They are part of the society and state, but are denied the same rights as others. This is segregation. x, 7, 9, 19t

Iran 47

Iraq 27t, 48

Ireland 29t, 42

Islam 4–5

growth of extremist versions of 32, 47–48

in Pakistan 35

Israeli/Palestinian conflict x, 1, 27t, 29t

Ivory Coast 8, 18

J

Japan

empire 3

Nanjing massacre 41

nationalization and militarization in 17

royal family 3

use of atomic bomb on 41

Jews 4, 16, 23

Nazi genocide of 28t, 42–43

in Romania 23, 38

K

Kashmir 10, 27t, 32
Khmer Rouge 28t, 43–44
King, Martin Luther 34

L

language
    elite 12
    in Tanzania 37, 38
Latvia 26t
Lebanon 8, 22, 48
Liberia 20
Lincoln, President Abraham 20
literacy 12

M

Malaysia 26t, 28t, 34
Mandela, Nelson 34
Mao Zedong 41
Marxism 11
memories 36
migration 7, 45, 46
military, expansion of European 12–13
Milosevic, Slobodan 32
minorities 7
    assimilation of x, 19, 19t, 21, 48–49
    nation-building and treatment of 18–24
    nationalism and uniting against 38–39
modernization: along with industrialization, as societies modernized they became more literate, more urban, and less bound by ancient traditions. States became stronger, and more was expected of them. In return, modern states demanded more from their citizens, included more of them in the political process, and tried to create a stronger sense of nationalism. Modernization has also weakened many old community ties and therefore created among some a sense of alienation and discomfort about the speed and nature of change. Modernity has spread unevenly, and there continues to be significant resistance to some of its aspects almost everywhere. 5–6, 12–13, 45
Monroe, President James 20
Mozambique 18
multiculturalism: a strategy for dealing with culturally distinct minorities within the state that allows each such group to follow its own practices and beliefs, in

return for which some loyalty to the state is expected. In modern nation-states, this implies that in return for such acceptance various minorities will recognize the legitimacy of the nation and be loyal to its nationalism. 21–22, 49

N

nation: a group of people who claim to have enough of a common culture to possess and live in their own sovereign state. Many nations do control such a sovereign state. Some ethnic groups claim to be a nation, yet do not have their own state. Such claims by a community within a state they do not consider their own can lead to severe conflicts. ix, 1

nation-state: a state in which the majority of people within it recognize it as their legitimate home, in which the majority feel that they identify with their state, and in which the majority feel they have enough in common with others living in the state to create a strong sense of unity.

nationalism: the sentiment that one owes allegiance to one's nation. Those who share a common nationalism feel a sense of kinship with others in the nation, even if they are not actually biologically related. A nationalist has no higher political loyalty than to his or her nation. ix, x, 5–6

unmixing and remixing of populations 46

using threat of danger to spur 31–32, 35, 38, 50

and variable identities 50

Native Americans 19, 21

Nazism: the Nazis were the German Fascist party that took power in 1933 when Adolf Hitler established his dictatorship. He persecuted and ultimately tried to exterminate Jews, invaded and, for a time, controlled most of Europe. Nazism and Germany were defeated and collapsed at the end of World War II in 1945. 17, 36, 42–43, 44

New Zealand 26t

Nigeria 8, 18, 26t

Northern Ireland ix–x, 9, 27t, 28t

Norway 29t

Nyerere, Julius 37

O

Ottoman Empire 2–3

ethnic cleansing of Armenians 16, 42

P

Pakistan 10

Islam in 35

national unity over dislike of India 35, 38

religious conflict in 48

state failures as a major cause of conflict 35–36

tribes in 24, 35

Palestinian/Israeli conflict x, 1, 27t, 29t

partitioning 29t

Poland 22–23

politics: the competition between groups for control of the power to allocate resources, determine how to govern their society, and decide what cultural values and habits will predominate. In states such groups are often organized on the basis of their economic interests, or class, and on different ideological conceptions of what is best for society as a whole. But they may also be based on competition between communities that identify themselves on the basis of kinship, ethnicity, religion, or just the region where they live. ix

Portugal 18

R

race: this is an ambiguous term that means different things in different parts of the world. In the United States it refers primarily to groups of people with different skin color, but elsewhere it can refer to ethnicities or even nations. Race is usually meant to refer to a common set of biological traits, but in practice it is actually a socially constructed category that generalizes about various ethnic groups. Prejudices based on such false assumptions are called racism. x, 16–17, 19

religion: a set of beliefs about higher, divine powers that rule the earth. Religious beliefs are an important part of any culture. Over time, local religious traditions have tended to be replaced by one of the major world religions, and this trend is continuing today. A term that has come into widespread use recently is "fundamentalism." It refers to adherents of one of the major world religions who claim to be going back to the original holy texts at the heart of their beliefs. ix, 2

S

U

United States of America
    affirmative action 49
    civil rights struggle 34
    Civil War 20, 28–29t, 32, 36–37
    conflict 26t
    fear of racial mixing in 44
    immigrants to 7, 21
    Native Americans 19, 21
    rallying of patriotic unity 31
    spread of nationalism in 14
    strategies for dealing with minorities 19–21, 49
    War of Independence 13

V

Vietnam
    and Cambodia 28t, 38, 43
    culture 2
    immigrants to U.S. 21
    promotion of nationalism 17

W

World War I 11, 16, 35
World War II 17
    causes of 35–36, 46
    and motives of revenge among Allies 41

Y

Yemen 48
Yugoslavia 22
    economic decline in 33
    mobilizing of Serb nationalism 32
    war in 17, 27t

An environmentally friendly book printed and bound in England by www.printondemand-worldwide.com